Mission Mathematics

Grades 9–12

Peggy House

Contributors

Mary Jo Aiken   Adele Hanson

Margaret Butler   Richard A. Hanson

Roger P. Day   Minot H. Parker

Alice Foster

Project Director

Michael C. Hynes

PUBLISHED IN COOPERATION WITH
THE NATIONAL AERONAUTICS AND
SPACE ADMINISTRATION

NATIONAL COUNCIL OF TEACHERS OF MATHEMATICS

Copyright © 1997 by
THE NATIONAL COUNCIL OF TEACHERS OF MATHEMATICS, INC.
1906 Association Drive, Reston, Virginia 20191-1593
All rights reserved

Library of Congress Cataloging-in-Publication Data
ISBN: 0-87353-436-0

Cover photograph by Greg Bock. Our galaxy, the Milky Way, with Jupiter and Sagittarius. Taken 20 July 1996 from Maroon Dam, Queensland, Australia; 15-minute exposure.

Text photographs, unless otherwise credited, are courtesy of NASA.

The publications of the National Council of Teachers of Mathematics present a variety of viewpoints. The views expressed or implied in this publication, unless otherwise noted, should not be interpreted as official positions of the Council.

PRINTED IN THE UNITED STATES OF AMERICA

CONTENTS

FOREWORD

Mission Mathematics: Linking Aerospace and the NCTM Standards is a collaborative project of the National Aeronautics and Space Administration (NASA) and the National Council of Teachers of Mathematics (NCTM). The vision of Frank Owen, director of educational programs for NASA, and James Gates, executive director of NCTM at the time of the conception of this project, initiated this unprecedented effort to link the science of aeronautics to the efforts of NCTM to develop standards for all aspects of mathematics education. The guidance of the project was entrusted to Pamela Mountjoy (NASA), Cynthia Rosso (NCTM), and Marilyn Hala (NCTM). Their support and expertise have facilitated the completion of the project, and their contributions have added immensely to the quality of the product.

Peggy House and her writing team have selected some exciting topics from the context of aerospace that will allow students an opportunity to explore some very interesting mathematics. The mathematics in the different activities does not represent the entirety of the high school mathematics curriculum or every application of mathematics to aerospace topics. Rather, the activities involve strategically selected aerospace topics that illustrate how this important science context can develop mathematical thinking using instruction based on the NCTM *Standards* documents: *Curriculum and Evaluation Standards for School Mathematics, Professional Standards for Teaching Mathematics,* and *Assessment Standards for School Mathematics.* The writing team for this book was instrumental in the conceptual design of the book, the writing of activities, and the researching of the literature to create an authentic link between aerospace and mathematics. The writing team consists of Mary Jo Aiken, Margaret Butler, Roger Day, Alice Foster, Adele Hanson, Richard Hanson, and Minot Parker.

The development of the activities for this project included pilot testing the activities in classrooms throughout the nation. NCTM made a call in the *NCTM News Bulletin* for teacher-participants in this phase of the project. We could never have anticipated the response from classroom teachers. Our e-mail was overloaded, and the regular mail always seemed to have another offer to volunteer time for the project. Many teachers telephoned us to follow up on their earlier correspondence. Clearly, our teachers are interested in using the context of aerospace to improve learning in their classrooms. Unfortunately, because of budget constraints in the project, we had to select only a few teacher-participants from the volunteers. The cost of duplicating pilot materials and the postage to deliver classroom sets to teachers prohibited us from using everyone who volunteered. For the pilot, classrooms were selected to give us a broad geographical, ethnic, and socioeconomic view of the effectiveness of the lessons. The large number of volunteers gave us the opportunity to do this well. For those teachers who participated by sending feedback from their classroom experience with draft activities, thank you. Your response allowed the writing teams to make the activities more effective for students. Also, we thank all of you who volunteered to assist in the project. This type of spirit makes the teaching profession very rewarding.

In addition, we would like to acknowledge the NASA staff who provided us with background information and materials.

As can be seen, this book was the product of many hands and minds. The collaborative effort of many people made this important project a reality. Thank you all.

Michael C. Hynes, Project Director

PREFACE

NASA is an organization built on vision: the vision to land humans on the Moon and return them safely to Earth, the vision to explore distant planets, the vision to peer deep into the depths of space and witness the birth of stars, the vision to construct a space station in orbit, the vision to create futures as yet unimagined.

NCTM also has a vision: a vision of a dynamic mathematics curriculum that promotes deep understanding of important mathematics and its uses; a vision of active, stimulating teaching and learning in environments that actively engage, challenge, and motivate students; a vision of ongoing assessment that is integral to, and aligned with, instruction; a vision of mathematical power and success for every child.

The visions of NASA and NCTM are highly compatible and complementary. From the context of aerospace arises important mathematics that can give students a glimpse into contemporary applications that are engaging and challenging, that permeate all aspects of modern life, and that invite students to become personally involved in open-ended investigations. These contemporary applications of mathematics, and the technology that makes them accessible to secondary school students, portray mathematics as dynamic and very much alive and well in the modern world. The mathematics of aerospace significantly furthers the goals expressed in NCTM's vision for mathematics education. At the same time, the attainment of NCTM's vision of mathematical power for every student will be essential if NASA is to find the next generation of mathematical thinkers needed to realize its ever-evolving vision of new futures.

During the development of *Mission Mathematics: Grades 9–12,* I was privileged to visit a number of NASA Space Centers and to meet with many members of the NASA staff engaged in all aspects of the aerospace enterprise. From the beginning, two characteristics of these people made a deep impression on me. First, each one exuded enthusiasm for the work he or she was doing; second, each clearly saw the importance of his or her work and its contribution to the total NASA mission.

The latter point is particularly significant. When young people think about the space program and their possible interest in it, the majority naturally think about being an astronaut. It is a response not unlike the dream of every high school player who has ever dribbled a basketball down the court to someday star in the NBA. Students have a level of understanding of what astronauts do; unfortunately, they lack insight into the vast array of important activities performed by the legion of professionals without whom there could be no astronauts. It is our hope that *Mission Mathematics: Grades 9–12* will introduce students to some of the exciting and significant ways in which mathematics might continue to engage them in whatever career paths they may ultimately choose.

In selecting topics for inclusion in this volume, we have been guided by the following goals:

◆ To present significant mathematics at a level attainable by high school students

◆ To engage students in reasoning and problem solving

◆ To lay a conceptual foundation for understanding mathematical ideas

◆ To show contemporary applications of mathematics in an important context and using contemporary methodologies

◆ To motivate and inspire

Mission Mathematics: Grades 9–12 strives to elucidate further the NCTM vision for meaningful mathematics, but that vision can come alive only in individual classrooms where the overall message, given consistently, is that no matter where students want to go in life, mathematics will help them get there. We hope that the materials in this volume will help teachers launch their students to a new level of mathematical awareness and interest.

In the predawn hours of 11 February 1997, as these materials were being readied for the press, I stood on the grounds of the Kennedy Space Center and watched the Space Shuttle *Discovery* light up the night sky as mission STS-82 lifted off Launch Pad 39A en route to its rendezvous with the Hubble Space Telescope. During the next ten days, astronauts made repairs and installed new technologies that will significantly improve Hubble's ability to expand our vision of the universe. On board *Discovery* with the astronauts was the mission patch illustrated on the covers of the three volumes in the Mission Mathematics series, a most fitting tribute to the partnership between NASA and NCTM that has made these materials possible and a timely lift-off for this project. The STS-82 astronauts accomplished their mission to expand the vision of the Hubble Space Telescope. Our mission to help students expand their vision of mathematics still lies before us. The launch was successful. The completion of the mission is in the hands of the teachers who accept the challenge to introduce their students to the vastness and wonder of the universe of mathematics.

We hope that you enjoy the journey.

SCALING UP

At night, when we gaze at the sky and marvel at the beauty of the twinkling stars, we often contemplate the vastness of the universe. But we have a difficult time conceptualizing the immensity of space. From an intellectual perspective, we can talk about the length of time it takes light to travel to Earth from these distant stars. We have learned in school that light travels at a speed of nearly 300 000 km/s; in a year, light travels 9.86×10^9 km. Light emanating from a star that is a light-year from Earth began its journey a year before we see it. Another way to think about this distance is to consider that we are seeing the star where it was a year ago. These intellectual musings make sense, but it is still difficult to get an intuitive notion of the vastness of space.

We are not the first to try to comprehend distances in the universe. Our natural human need to understand the world around us has prompted many people throughout history to search for answers to their questions about the size of our universe. More than two thousand years ago, scientists in ancient Greece were using the known mathematics of the day to estimate the distance to the Moon and the Sun. As new mathematics was invented, our ability to measure these distances improved. But it was not until the seventeenth century that Cassini determined the first reasonably accurate calculation of the distance from Earth to the Sun. Using more refined mathematics and improved technology, humans have continued to measure the distances between celestial bodies. As the age of space exploration began, distances in the universe became the province of all kinds of people, not just scientists. Daily newspapers printed reports of manned and unmanned space ventures, comic books carried fictitious stories about interstellar travel, and school books began to include more data about the universe.

It is rather ordinary and routine in these times to hear about satellite launches and Space Shuttle missions. Men and women traveling in orbit high above Earth seem very far away. The pictures taken by Shuttle astronauts from more than 100 miles in space make Earth seem small. It is interesting to note that if Earth were an orange, these astronauts would be no farther from the edible part of the orange than the outer edge of the skin. Again, these notions are difficult to consider because of the vastness of space and the size of planets and stars.

NASA reports to us about the travels of unmanned space vehicles, such as *Pioneer 10, Voyager 1,* and *Voyager 2.* These spacecraft have traveled for years to reach a distance of more than 5 billion miles from Earth and are continuing on journeys that may last well into the next millennium. With these unmanned spacecraft, humankind is searching for the boundary of the solar system, the *heliopause.* This edge of the solar system may be 9 to 11 trillion miles from Earth. As spacecraft have made their way through the solar system, scientists have learned a great deal about the planets from data sent back to NASA laboratories. This type of NASA exploration helps scientists learn more and more about the universe.

Because of humankind's continuing fascination with the mysteries of space, it becomes even more important that all citizens gain insight into the size and nature of the solar system. We must begin to scale up our understanding of sizes and distances in the context of space.

SCALING THE HEIGHTS

Looking out into the vastness of space, we cannot help but marvel at the enormous sizes and distances of bodies in our universe. But it is hard for students to comprehend just how large and how far away are the objects in our solar system and beyond, although an understanding of such magnitudes is important for the other activities in *Mission Mathematics: Grades 9–12*. Thus, we begin with this unit on scaling as a way to help students put measurements in perspective.

PURPOSES

This unit gives students models that help them conceptualize the magnitudes of measurements in aerospace applications. The activities reinforce concepts of ratio and proportion and afford opportunities to apply estimation strategies and proportional reasoning.

INTRODUCTION

The unit begins with a set of activities that focus on scale models of the solar system and emphasize important concepts of ratio and proportion. Students should do these activities before they undertake the later units of *Mission Mathematics*. As written, the activities presume the use of a spreadsheet because that is a natural tool with which to undertake the calculations; however, the activities can also be done with a calculator.

Measurements in the included tables are given in units commonly used by NASA scientists and others. Sometimes they are metric units; at other times they are customary units. You are free to choose to work in one or both systems, but in any event, students should develop a sense of the orders of magnitudes of sizes and distances. You should also engage students in discussion about accuracy versus approximations and why many of the numbers are rounded to thousands or even millions. You will also encounter some new units that may be unfamiliar to the students, such as an *astronomical unit* (AU) or a *light-year* (lt-yr), which they should recognize as measures of distance, not time.

It is also important to discuss the simplifying assumptions that are made in this unit. For the sake of the activities, we assume that planetary orbits are circular and coplanar, and we use average distances from the Sun. Students who are familiar with the conic sections can construct ellipses to match the eccentricities of some planetary orbits and compare them with the graphs of circles. Since the eccentricities (see table 1) are quite close to zero, students should be able to see why the approximation with circular orbits is a reasonable first step. A later unit in *Mission Mathematics*, "Modeling Elliptical Orbits," allows more advanced students to refine their orbits to include ellipses.

MODELING THE SOLAR SYSTEM

The scaling activities begin by having students consider only the relative sizes of the planets by making comparisons with familiar objects. They will find, for example, that if Earth is represented by a basketball, Jupiter will be nearly 270 centimeters in diameter and the Sun, more than 26 meters. In contrast, if the basketball represents the Sun, Earth shrinks to less than 0.25 centimeter. Use this opportunity to ask, "What if...?" Trying a number of such comparisons is easy with a spreadsheet. Students can then be challenged to locate a set of physical objects to represent one of their scales. Having completed this part of the activity, students will find the information on the distribution of matter in the solar system easier to comprehend.

Curriculum Connections:
  Ratio and Proportions
  Geometry
  Modeling
  Data

Related *Mission Mathematics* Activities: *These activities find a natural extension in the unit "Modeling Elliptical Orbits."*

Teaching Tip: *Because doing the calculations with a calculator is somewhat tedious, you may want to have different groups of students complete different parts of the tables and pool their results.*

Teaching Tip: *The student pages include data tables with planetary sizes and distances. Such information is also readily available from numerous publications and Internet sites. This activity offers a good opportunity for student inquiry, and you may prefer to have your class research the data themselves rather than be given the tables.*

Assessment Tip: *Students can demonstrate their understanding by making bulletin-board displays or by constructing physical models of their comparisons.*

Teaching Tip: *This is a good context in which to discuss the concept of significant figures in measurements.*

Next, students are asked to scale the mean distances from the Sun to each planet. This activity in itself usually presents little difficulty. But when students are asked to use a single scale to accommodate *both* size *and* distance, the problem becomes much more complex. Students soon recognize that any distance scale that might fit on, for example, a piece of paper or the chalkboard will require that the planets be too small to construct or even see. A scale of reasonable planetary sizes will probably not fit in the classroom or even the school.

Table 1 gives relevant solar system data taken from NASA charts. Values computed by students may vary slightly because of rounding.

Table 1
Solar System Data

Body	Equatorial diameter (km)	Equatorial diameter (mi)	Diameter with reference to Earth	Mean solar dist. (M km)	Mean solar dist. (M mi)	Mean solar dist. (AU)	Orbital period (Earth years)	Eccentricity	T^2 (T in years)	R^3 (R in AU)	T^2/R^3 (Kepler's 3rd Law)
Mercury	4 880	3 026	0.38	57.9	35.9	0.39	0.2	0.206	0.06	0.06	0.98
Venus	12 100	7 502	0.95	108.2	67.1	0.72	0.6	0.007	0.38	0.37	1.01
Earth	12 756	7 909	1.00	149.6	92.8	1.0	1.0	0.017	1.00	1.00	1.00
Mars	6 794	4 212	0.53	227.9	141.3	1.52	1.9	0.093	3.54	3.51	1.01
Jupiter	143 200	88 784	11.23	778.3	482.5	5.2	11.9	0.048	140.66	140.61	1.00
Saturn	120 536	74 732	9.45	1 427	884.7	9.55	29.5	0.056	867.89	870.98	1.00
Uranus	51 800	32 116	4.06	2 871	1 780.0	19.22	84.0	0.046	7 057.68	7 100.03	0.99
Neptune	49 528	30 707	3.88	4 497	2 788.1	31.11	164.8	0.009	27 155.74	30 109.26	0.90
Pluto	2 330	1 445	0.18	5 914	3 666.7	39.44	247.7	0.248	61 355.29	61 349.46	1.00
Moon	3 476	2 155	0.27	* 0.38	* 0.2			0.055			
Sun	1 392 000	863 040	109.13								

* from Earth

REACHING OUT

The "Reaching Out" activity on student page 11 supplies important background information for the later unit on communicating through space; you can use it either as part of the scaling unit or as an introduction to the communications unit. The important realization is that when we are dealing with distances in space, even light, which travels at 186 000 miles per second, may take millions of years to reach Earth.

Interplanetary communications and travel are affected by the relative positions of the planets as they orbit the Sun. Students need to be able to visualize the geometry of several planets orbiting the Sun at different velocities. Even though we make several simplifying assumptions, such as coplanar circular orbits, the differences in the maximum and minimum distances between two planets can be dramatic. You can, of course, extend the consideration to elliptical orbits if you choose.

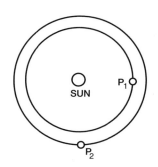

Fig. 1. Orbits around the Sun

Dynamic geometry software offers a simple but effective illustration of the relative motions of orbiting planets. By constructing several concentric circles and a point, or "planet," on each and using the "animate" or "animation" command, students can make the points move in their respective orbits at varying speeds. Students will quickly see how two planets get in and out of sync with each other (fig. 1). They should then be able to deduce the following procedures to calculate the minimum and maximum distances from Earth to each planet.

     Mission Mathematics: Grades 9–12

Solutions:

		Min. Dist.	Max. Dist
(a) P orbit between E and S; P and E same side of S		$r(E) - r(P)$	
(b) P orbit between E and S; P and E opposite sides of S			$r(E) + r(P)$
(c) E orbit between P and S; P and E same side of S		$r(P) - r(E)$	
(d) E orbit between P and S; P and E opposite sides of S			$r(P) + r(E)$

Here $r(E)$ and $r(P)$ are the mean distances of Earth and the planet from the Sun. Table 2 gives approximations of the minimum and maximum distances between Earth and the other planets in millions of kilometers.

Table 2
Distances between Earth and Other Planets

Body	Min. distance from Earth	Max. distance from Earth
Mercury	91.7	207.5
Venus	41.4	257.8
Mars	78.3	377.5
Jupiter	628.7	927.9
Saturn	1277.4	1576.6
Uranus	2721.4	3020.6
Neptune	4347.4	4646.6
Pluto	5764.4	6063.6

Some examples of what these distances mean are shown in table 3.

Table 3
Travel Times from Earth

Destination	From Earth by jet (600 mph)	From Earth by rocket (25 000 mph)	From Earth at speed of light (186 000 mi/sec)
Mercury	10 yr 10 mo	3 mo	5 min
Venus	5 yr 5 mo	1.5 mo	2.5 min
Mars	8 yr 10 mo	2.5 mo	4 min
Jupiter	74 yr 3 mo	1 yr 9 mo	35 min
Saturn	150 yr 5 mo	3 yr 7 mo	1 h 11 min
Uranus	318 yr 6 mo	7 yr 7 mo	2 h 30 min
Neptune	513 yr 2 mo	12 yr 3 mo	4 h 2 min
Pluto	690 yr 1 mo	16 yr 5 mo	5 h 25 min
Moon	16.5 da	9.4 hr	1.2 sec
Sun	17 yr 8 mo	4 mo	8.5 min
Alpha Centauri	$4.8(10^6)$ yr	114 155.2 yr	4.2 yr
Sirius	$9.6(10^6)$ yr	228 310.4 yr	8.4 yr

LAUNCH WINDOWS

Given the vast distances of space illustrated in the previous activities, we next turn to the question of determining launch windows. The foregoing simulation of two planets orbiting at different speeds sets the stage for a consideration of the mathematics of planning a launch to Mars. When launch windows are discussed in this context, two considerations come into play: First, a "daily window" occurs during which a rocket launched from Florida will be on a proper "outward" heading. Suppose that such a window exists between 10 A.M. and noon. It is easy to see that during that same two-hour period, a rocket launched from the opposite side of the globe would be headed in the wrong direction. Likewise, because of the rotation of Earth on its axis, after a period of some hours a rocket launched from Florida will also be headed in the wrong direction.

The second type of launch window arises from the relative positions of Earth and Mars in their orbits. As the previous activities have shown, at times Mars is too far from Earth and in the wrong location relative to the Sun. Thus, launches must be timed to coincide with proper planetary alignment. Such planning requires much mathematics. Consider, for example, that the *Galileo* probe was launched from the Space Shuttle on 18 October 1989 and arrived precisely at its destination, Jupiter, on 7 December 1995!

Mathematical Connections: *Here are the distances to some of the brightest stars, given in light-years:*

Canopus	*98 lt-yr*
Rigel	*910 lt-yr*
Betelgeuse	*510 lt-yr*
Antares	*330 lt-yr*
Pollux	*36 lt-yr*
Deneb	*1800 lt-yr*

For each star, find out what was happening on Earth when the light that you see tonight began its journey.

Assessment Tip: *Pose questions such as these:*

- *Where will Earth and Mars be after 27 months? After 28 months?*
- *When is the next time that the separation angle will be zero?*
- *Approximately where in the orbits will that separation angle occur?*

This activity concerns the second type of launch window. Students can use a spreadsheet to model the relative positions of Earth and Mars first under simplified initial conditions and later in more complex settings. They also can use the information from their spreadsheets to model the locations of the two planets geometrically. Since Earth completes one orbit of 360 degrees around the Sun in one year, Earth moves about 0.99 degree per day; Mars, which orbits the Sun in 1.88 Earth years or approximately 687 Earth days, advances in its orbit about 0.52 degree per day. Figure 2 was constructed with the Geometer's Sketchpad using data compiled in a spreadsheet. It represents the positions of Earth and Mars after 18, 19, ..., 26 months, if we assume that both planets were aligned along the positive *x*-axis at the start of the first month (1 January). The corresponding data from the spreadsheet are shown in table 4.

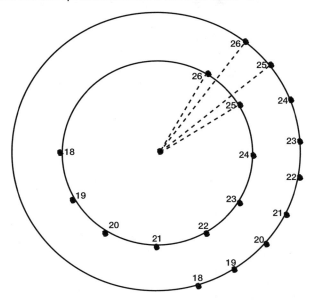

Fig. 2. A representation of the relative positions of Earth and Mars after 18, 19, ..., 26 months

Table 4
Positions of Earth and Mars

Date	Months elapsed	Days elapsed	Location of Earth (degrees)	Location of Mars (degrees)
1 July	18	546	178.5	286.1
1 Aug.	19	577	209.1	302.4
1 Sept.	20	608	239.7	318.6
1 Oct.	21	638	269.3	334.3
1 Nov.	22	669	299.8	350.6
1 Dec.	23	699	329.4	6.3
1 Jan.	24	730	0.0	22.5
1 Feb.	25	761	30.6	38.8
1 Mar.	26	789	58.2	53.4

From the spreadsheet and graphic we see the following:

- About 22.5 months (687 days) after the 1 January "start" (i.e., in mid-November), Mars has completed its first orbit and returned to its initial position on the positive *x*-axis. At the same time, Earth has completed one orbit plus approximately 318 degrees of its second orbit. Earth now "trails" Mars by about 42 degrees.

- Two years after the 1 January "start," again on 1 January, Earth has completed two orbits and is now back to its initial position on the positive *x*-axis. Mars has moved forward to a position 22.5 degrees from the positive *x*-axis. Earth, which is moving faster than Mars, has closed the gap to 22.5 degrees after 24 months.

- After 25 months, Earth is about 8 degrees "behind" Mars; after 26 months, Earth has overtaken Mars and is about 5 degrees "ahead" of it. Sometime during that period, the phase angle between the two has again closed to 0 degrees, although when that happened they were both about 48 degrees beyond the positive *x*-axis. The alignment occurred on about 19 February.

Once again, these models have made simplifying assumptions, among them the presumption of circular orbits and constant orbital velocities. In fact, with elliptical orbits, planets travel faster when they are near the Sun (the focus) and more slowly when they are far away. These simplifying assumptions, however, enable us to understand the mathematics of what is happening without introducing unnecessarily complex mathematics.

Teaching Tip: *Encourage interested students to engage in further inquiry by removing some of the simplifying assumptions. For example, ask them to model this problem using elliptical orbits.*

Mars Views

MODELING THE SOLAR SYSTEM

The solar system—our Sun, its nine planets, their moons, and other orbiting bodies—can be described only in measurements of millions, and even hundreds of millions, of miles or kilometers. With such numbers, it is hard for us to comprehend the enormous size of objects and the vast distances between them. But we can get a better sense of size and distance by scaling down these objects to more familiar measurements and evaluating the relative proportions of our models. Such scaling is not difficult if we enlist the aid of a spreadsheet or the table functions of a calculator.

Scaling Planetary Sizes

The table below gives information about the equatorial diameters of the Sun, the planets, and our Moon. Note that because a planet rotates on its axis, it is not perfectly spherical. Instead, the planet bulges slightly at its equator and is somewhat flattened at the poles. For example, Earth's equatorial diameter is 12 756 kilometers (7909 miles), whereas its polar diameter is 12 714 kilometers (7883 miles). However, because the difference is so small compared with the size of Earth, we are justified in treating the planet as though it is a sphere. In fact, in most computations involving the size of Earth, we will round these measurements even further.

Copy the information from the table into your spreadsheet and then complete the next two columns of the table by doing the following:

◆ Use your spreadsheet to calculate the diameters of the planets, the Sun, and the Moon in miles. Remember that 1 mile equals 1.61 kilometers and 1 kilometer equals 0.62 mile.

◆ Calculate the ratio of the diameters of the other bodies compared with Earth's diameter. How many Plutos are needed to line up across the diameter of Earth? Of Saturn? How many Earths would it take to line up across the diameter of Jupiter? Of the Sun?

The Exploration Begins

Suppose that you want to make a model of our solar system in which Earth is represented by a basketball and the Sun, the Moon, and the other planets are all proportional. Use your spreadsheet or calculator and complete a column titled "Solar System Diameters Scaled to 'Earth = Basketball.'" The diameter of a basketball is 24 centimeters.

The Solar System: Sizes				
Body	Equatorial Diameter (kilometers)	Equatorial Diameter (miles)	Diameter Compared with Earth's	Solar System Diameters Scaled to …
Mercury	4 880			
Venus	12 100			
Earth	12 756		1	
Mars	6 794			
Jupiter	143 200			
Saturn	120 536			
Uranus	51 800			
Neptune	49 528			
Pluto	2 330			
Moon	3 476			
Sun	1 392 000			

After you determine the diameters of the other bodies, find objects that you could use to represent each one and add their names to your table.

◆ Think of all the spheres you have ever seen. If the smallest sphere represents the smallest planet, what could you find to represent the other planets? Would the Sun fit into your classroom?

◆ Add several columns to your table, similar to the "Solar System Diameters Scaled to ..." column, and change the scale each time. For example, you might decide that the basketball should represent the Sun, or you might let one of the planets be the size of a marble. Remember, you are trying to show the *relative sizes* of those bodies. Try to locate a set of physical objects that you can bring into the classroom to illustrate one of your models.

◆ On a large local or state map, locate the two landmarks or cities that are farthest apart. Use the distance between those places to represent the diameter of Jupiter and then scale the diameters of the other planets, the Moon, and the Sun. Name the landmarks or cities at the endpoints of each diameter. For example, in the state of Wisconsin, the diameter of Jupiter would be represented by the distance from Kenosha to Superior and the diameter of Earth would be represented by the distance from Kenosha to Milwaukee.

Scaling Planetary Distances

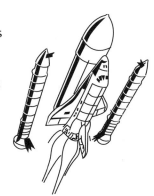

In addition to scaling the sizes of the planets and other bodies, we are concerned with their relative distances from the Sun. But before we examine planetary distances, we must become familiar with the work of the German astronomer Johannes Kepler (1571–1630).

Before Kepler, the Polish astronomer Nicolaus Copernicus had published in 1543 his theory that the planets revolve around the Sun in circular orbits. But Kepler had access to a voluminous set of very accurate observations of the stars and planets, and by studying those data, he was forced to conclude that the planetary orbits could not be circular. At the time, Kepler's abandonment of the theory of circular orbits was considered extremely radical; nonetheless, he published three laws of planetary motion, the first two in 1609 and the third in 1619, that changed astronomy and physics forever. Kepler's laws state the following:

I. The planets revolve around the Sun in elliptical orbits with the Sun at one focus of the ellipse.

II. A line joining the planet to the Sun will sweep over equal areas in equal periods of time.

III. The square of the period of a planet—the time it takes to make one complete orbit—is proportional to the cube of its average distance from the Sun.

A greatly exaggerated diagram of an elliptical orbit is shown on the next page, along with common terminology and symbolism. In this diagram, the eccentricity of the ellipse is about 0.75, giving it a very elongated shape. In reality, however, the orbits of the planets are much more

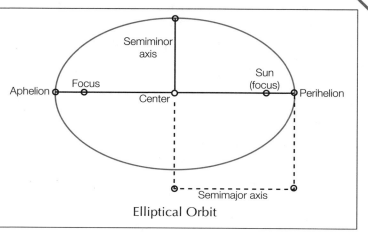

Aphelion: The point on the orbit farthest from the Sun

Perihelion: The point on the orbit nearest to the Sun

Focal distance (*c*): The distance from the center to either focus

Semimajor axis (*a*): Half the length of the major axis

Semiminor axis (*b*): Half the length of the minor axis

Eccentricity (*e*): The ratio of the focal distance to the semimajor axis ($e = c/a$)

Elliptical Orbit

circular. The next figure is a much closer approximation of the shape of Earth's orbit. The accompanying table gives the eccentricities of all the planetary orbits.

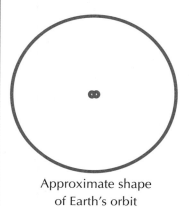

Approximate shape of Earth's orbit

Body	Eccentricity
Mercury	0.206
Venus	0.007
Earth	0.017
Mars	0.093
Jupiter	0.048
Saturn	0.056
Uranus	0.046
Neptune	0.009
Pluto	0.248
Moon	0.055

In a later unit of *Mission Mathematics*, you can explore how to model elliptical orbits, but for the present we simplify our exploration by assuming that the planetary orbits are circular. Why is it reasonable to make that assumption?

◆ The table below gives the *mean distances* of the planets from the Sun. Copy the information into your spreadsheet. Since you may be more accustomed to thinking about distances in miles, calculate the mean solar distances in millions of miles.

◆ An *astronomical unit* (AU) is equal to the mean distance from Earth to the Sun. It is common to use the Earth-Sun distance as a measuring stick for expressing other distances in space. Use your spreadsheet to calculate the distances from the other planets to the Sun

Body	Mean Solar Distance (millions of kilometers)	Mean Solar Distance (millions of miles)	Mean Solar Distance (astronomical units)	Orbital Period (Earth years)
Mercury	57.9			0.24
Venus	108.2			0.62
Earth	149.6		1	1.00
Mars	227.9			1.88
Jupiter	778.3			11.86
Saturn	1427			29.46
Uranus	2871			84.01
Neptune	4497			164.79
Pluto	5914			247.70
Moon (distance from Earth)	0.38			

The Solar System: Distances

in astronomical units. In other words, find the ratios of the planet-Sun distances to the Earth-Sun distance.

◆ Obtain a large map of North America and measure the distance from Seattle, Washington, to Miami, Florida. Let that distance represent the mean distance from the Sun to Pluto. Assume that you have placed a model of the Sun at Miami (where else?). Draw the orbits of the other planets. Name the cities that you could visit on a trip from planet to planet. Identify the scale that you developed in inches-to-millions-of-miles and in centimeters-to-millions-of-kilometers.

Continuing the Mission

◆ Making a scale model of planetary sizes *or* planetary distances is much easier than making a single model of planetary sizes *and* distances. Select a single ratio and use it to make a physical model of the solar system showing both size and distance to scale. For example, if you use the earlier scale in which a basketball represented Earth, determine appropriate sizes 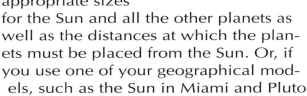 for the Sun and all the other planets as well as the distances at which the planets must be placed from the Sun. Or, if you use one of your geographical models, such as the Sun in Miami and Pluto

in Seattle, determine how big each planet will be and where it will be located.

◆ The Space Shuttle and other manned spacecraft normally orbit about 100 to 200 miles above Earth. Where would such an orbiting spacecraft be located in your model of the solar system?

◆ Why does Kepler's second law lead to the conclusion that the planets must be traveling faster in their orbits when they are closer to the Sun and more slowly when they are farther from the Sun?

◆ Use the data in the last table and your spreadsheet to demonstrate Kepler's third law. Use mean distances in astronomical units and orbital periods in years.

◆ Write a description of what you have learned about the relative sizes and distances of objects in our solar system. What surprised you the most?

Reaching Out

On 20 July 1969, the astronaut Neil Armstrong stepped onto the surface of the Moon, the first human to set foot on another world. The mission, which included a number of orbits of Earth, travel time to and from the Moon, and twenty-six hours on the lunar surface, took just over eight days from launch to splashdown. To break out of low Earth orbit (LEO) enroute to the Moon, the *Apollo* spacecraft had to achieve a velocity of just over 24 000 miles per hour.

Perhaps because we have become accustomed to science fiction in movies and on television, where starships are assumed to travel at impossible speeds, we often do not appreciate the magnitude of the time necessary to traverse the enormous distances even within our solar system and certainly beyond our immediate "neighborhood." We can get a better understanding of such magnitudes by considering the travel times required to reach out to other planets.

Think about two planets in orbit around the Sun. Assume for simplicity that they are in circular orbit. As you can tell from the diagram, the distance between the planets will vary considerably depending on whether the planets are on the same side or on opposite sides of the Sun.

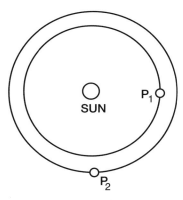

◆ Study the diagram and determine how you can calculate the distance from Earth to another planet for each of these situations:

(a) The planet's orbit is between Earth and the Sun, and the planet and Earth are on the same side of the Sun.

(b) The planet's orbit is between Earth and the Sun, and the planet and Earth are on opposite sides of the Sun.

(c) Earth's orbit is between the planet and the Sun and the planet and Earth are on the same side of the Sun.

(d) Earth's orbit is between the planet and the Sun, and the planet and Earth are on opposite sides of the Sun.

◆ You can get a good idea of how the distance between planets changes by modeling their motion with such software as the Geometer's Sketchpad or Cabri Geometry II. To do this, construct two or more concentric circles, "orbits," of different radii. Construct a point, or "planet," on each circle, and use the "animate" or "animation" command to move the planets around their respective orbits. Vary the speeds of animation to see how the planets get in and out of alignment with each other.

◆ Using your calculator or spreadsheet and the following table of distances of the planets from the Sun, calculate the minimum and maximum distances between Earth and each planet. Note that we are again making a simplifying assumption by treating this activity as if

Body	Mean Solar Distance (millions of kilometers)	Minimum Distance from Earth (millions of kilometers)	Maximum Distance from Earth (millions of kilometers)
Mercury	57.9		
Venus	108.2		
Earth	149.6	N/A	N/A
Mars	227.9		
Jupiter	778.3		
Saturn	1427		
Uranus	2871		
Neptune	4497		
Pluto	5914		
Moon (distance from Earth)	0.38	N/A	N/A

all the planets lie in the same orbital plane. Although this approach affects the calculations somewhat, the results will be adequate for our purposes.

✦ A jet airplane travels at speeds of about 600 miles, or 960 kilometers, per hour; a rocket escaping Earth's gravity might travel at 25 000 miles, or 40 000 kilometers, per hour; light travels at 186 000 miles per second. Add columns to your spreadsheet to determine how long it would take to reach each of the other planets if you could—

- travel by jet;
- travel by rocket;
- travel at the speed of light.

How long does it take light from the Sun to reach each planet?

✦ Why is it accurate to say that when you look into the sky, you are looking back in time?

✦ Look up the distances from Earth to several stars or galaxies visible in the sky with either a telescope or the naked eye. What was happening on Earth when the light you see from these bodies tonight left on its journey to Earth? When the light we see tonight left the Pleiades, Kepler had not yet published his laws of planetary motion!

At the speed of light, light from these bodies …	will reach Earth in …
Sirius (Dog Star)	8.4 years
Pleiades star cluster	400 years
Crab Nebula	4 000 years
Center of Milky Way	38 000 years
Nearest galaxy, Andromeda	2.2 million years

The *Mars Observer* spacecraft passed another milestone toward launch when it was moved from the Payload Hazardous Servicing facility on Kennedy Space Center to Launch Complex 40 on Cape Canaveral Air Force Station and mated to the Martin Marietta *Titan III* rocket. With the payload atop the launch vehicle, checks of the *Mars Observer* spacecraft and the attached Transfer Orbit Stage (TOS) will begin this weekend.... All activities are currently on schedule to support a launch at the opening of the Mars planetary opportunity on September 16. The launch window extends from 1:02 to 3:05 P.M. EDT.

Mars Observer will be the first U.S. mission to Mars since the Viking program in 1975. From a circular Martian polar orbit of 250 miles, it will create a detailed global portrait of the planet. The spacecraft will map the surface and study Mars geology while profiling its atmosphere and weather. The mission is designed to span one Martian year, or 687 Earth days.

Press release from Kennedy Space Center
12 August 1992

When NASA plans to launch a mission, all orbital maneuvers are carefully timed and are based on a set of conditions that must be present at the time of launch. If the launch is delayed to the point at which conditions have changed so much that the mission cannot continue as designed, NASA either must scrap the mission or wait until the necessary conditions again prevail.

The *Mars Observer* spacecraft was originally scheduled to launch on 16 September 1992. After a delay caused by contamination on the surface of the spacecraft, *Mars Observer* was successfully launched on 25 September. Had the mission missed its launch window, which would have expired on 13 October, scientists would have had to wait another two years before launch conditions would again be acceptable. One factor in timing those launch conditions is the relative position of the planets in their orbits. Since Earth completes one full revolution of the Sun in 365 days and Mars completes one full revolution in 687 days, the planets obviously do not maintain the same alignment as they move through their orbital paths around the Sun.

Because travel times to Mars have varied from just over four months to almost a year, a spacecraft launched from Earth must be placed in a trajectory that will take it not to where Mars *is* but to where Mars *will be* at the time of arrival. This is analogous to a quarterback who throws a long pass to a receiver downfield. The quarterback must anticipate where the receiver will be when the football arrives and aim the pass accordingly.

NASA's Exploration of Mars			
Spacecraft	Launch	Arrival	Nature of Mission
Mariner 4	11/28/64	07/14/65	Flyby
Mariner 6	02/24/69	07/31/69	Flyby
Mariner 7	03/27/69	08/05/69	Flyby
Mariner 9	05/30/71	11/13/71	Mars orbit
Viking 1	08/20/75	07/19/76	Orbit and landing
Viking 2	09/09/75	08/07/76	Orbit and landing
Mars Observer	09/25/92	08/24/93?	Orbit*

*NASA lost contact with the *Mars Observer* on 8/21/93, three days before it was to fire its main rocket engines and decelerate into orbit. The fate of the spacecraft remains unknown.

✦ If you have not already done so, complete the activity on modeling planets traveling in different orbits using such software as the Geometer's Sketchpad or Cabri Geometry II (see student page 12). This activity will help you visualize the situation of Earth in an inner orbit completing one revolution in 365 days and Mars in an outer orbit completing one revolution in 687 days.

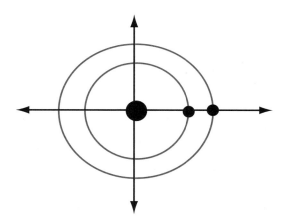

✦ You can set up a two-dimensional Cartesian-coordinate model of the orbits of Earth and Mars around the Sun. For simplicity, assume that the orbital paths are circular and in the same plane. Design your model on the basis of the following guidelines:

• Let the Sun be located at the origin, and construct two concentric circles, with centers at the origin, to represent the orbits of Earth and Mars. Select appropriate radii for these circles proportional to the average distance of each planet from the Sun. See the chart of distances on student page 10.

• Assume initially that launch conditions are such that both planets lie on the positive x-axis and that launch occurs on 1 January. Remember that all our assumptions are made to simplify the model; once the model is working, we can add the complexities of launching on other dates and from different relative positions.

✦ Use a spreadsheet, such as the one below, to calculate the angular motion of Earth and Mars around the Sun through two complete years. Plot the location of each planet on the first day of each month for the two-year period.

Date	Days Elapsed	Earth's Position (degrees)	Mars's Position (degrees)
1 Jan.	0	0	0
1 Feb.	31		
1 Mar.	59		
1 Apr.			
1 May			
1 June			

• Through how many degrees does Earth move in one day?

• Through how many degrees does Mars move in one day?

• Write the equations of the circles that represent your orbital paths of Earth and Mars. Explain how you determined what the radii should be.

• Six months after launch, where will each planet be?

• When Earth crosses the positive y-axis for the first time, where will Mars be? Explain how you decided on this location.

• How long will it take for Mars to cross the negative x-axis? At that time, where will Earth be?

• By the time Earth has completed one full orbit, where will Mars be?

• By the time Mars has completed one full orbit, where will Earth be? How many orbits around the Sun will Earth have completed?

• We assumed that both planets were initially on the positive x-axis; at that time their angular separation was 0 degrees. When Mars has completed one orbit, what will be the angular separation of Earth and Mars?

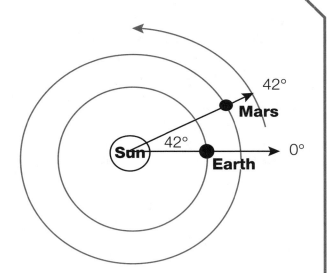

◆ When the *Mars Observer* was launched in September 1992, the two planets, Earth and Mars, were not actually lined up in a straight line from the Sun, as we assumed in the previous activity. Rather, a 42-degree phase angle existed between them. In other words, the central angle formed by connecting the location of each planet to the Sun was 42 degrees. To provide a reference point from which to model this situation, assume that Earth starts at an angle of 0 degrees and Mars starts at an angle of 42 degrees to the positive *x*-axis, with both planets moving in a counterclockwise direction. Modify your spreadsheet to track the relative positions of the two planets, starting on 25 September 1992, and determine the next two times the planets are in the same relative alignment.

◆ In creating these simulations, we have oversimplified the problem to make it easier to analyze. Describe at least one factor that we have ignored in our simulation but that we definitely would have to consider if we were actually trying to predict accurately the next launch-window opportunity.

◆ Write a paragraph explaining why it is not possible to launch spacecraft to Mars "just any old time." Use charts or diagrams to support your explanation.

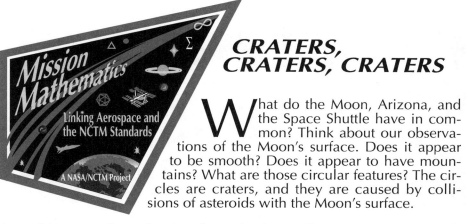

Mission Mathematics
Linking Aerospace and the NCTM Standards
A NASA/NCTM Project

CRATERS, CRATERS, CRATERS

What do the Moon, Arizona, and the Space Shuttle have in common? Think about our observations of the Moon's surface. Does it appear to be smooth? Does it appear to have mountains? What are those circular features? The circles are craters, and they are caused by collisions of asteroids with the Moon's surface.

Asteroids are rocks or hunks of metal orbiting the Sun. Many asteroids travel their paths between the orbits of Mars and Jupiter. Thousands of these asteroids—many are large enough to be seen with a medium-sized telescope—have been observed, named, and cataloged by scientists. At times, these asteroids collide, often resulting in pieces that are thrown out of their orbits and begin a collision path with other planets and moons. As can be seen, many asteroids have collided with the surface of the Moon, and the craters can be very large.

Yes, Arizona has a crater of some note. Barringer Crater is one of the best examples in the United States of a collision of an asteroid with Earth's surface. This particular crater is 1.2 kilometers in diameter and 180 meters deep. Scientists think that a meteorite—an asteroid that enters Earth's atmosphere—up to 60 meters in diameter and weighing about 900 million kilograms slammed into Earth to form the crater. It is estimated that the explosion caused by the impact was equivalent to a 15-megaton bomb explosion. Scientists use this crater and a more recently formed one in Siberia to estimate the effect that another collision of the same magnitude would have on our planet. Some scientific evidence links an earlier collision with the extinction of the dinosaurs, raising some concern about the possibe catastrophic result of a future collision.

Astronauts on the Shuttle orbiter need to be concerned about another type of material in space. Human-made objects also orbit Earth. This "space junk," or orbital debris, comes in many sizes. Many particles are very small, but even tiny paint flecks can be dangerous because they travel at very high speeds. In fact, at least one Shuttle has been hit by one of these particles. The impact of a fleck of paint made a crater in the orbiter window. Yes, the Shuttle—at least one of them—had a crater. Fortunately, the window was thick enough to withstand the blow.

Since orbital debris, even in its smallest form, is a danger to future missions, NASA scientists are working on the problem from many angles. For example, as you can surmise, "space junk" is a danger to astronauts performing EVA (extra-vehicular activities). If a particle should hit the astronaut, it would certainly puncture the space suit and cause it to depressurize. Scientists are cataloging the large pieces so future satellites and Shuttle missions are not placed in their paths. In some instances, Shuttles have been maneuvered to avoid a collision with orbital debris. In addition, designers of space suits are working to find better materials and designs to resist punctures. Backup systems are available to help an astronaut return to the orbiter if he or she is hit by orbital debris. Scientists at the Johnson Space Center's Hypervelocity Impact Test Facility (HITF) are firing small missiles to determine the effects of high-velocity impact on different materials, including those used to make the skin of the Space Shuttle.

The success of these projects and other important NASA laboratory work will improve the margin of safety for future space missions.

Moon

MODELING ORBITAL DEBRIS PROBLEMS

The problem of space pollution caused by human-made debris in orbit is presented as a context for studying mathematical modeling. This unit should help students realize that not all problems are solvable with precise measurements and exact answers but that mathematical models enable us to look at trends and to make predictions about probable outcomes. The ambiguity of some of these activities may be frustrating to a few students, but it reflects the realities with which mathematicians and scientists must work.

PURPOSES

In this unit, students create and compare various mathematical models as a way to investigate some of the questions raised by the proliferation of orbital debris. Although the models are greatly simplified to make them understandable to high school students, they offer insight into the process of mathematical modeling and its importance. Throughout the unit it is assumed that your students will work with appropriate technology. Depending on what you have available and what you prefer, these tools may include graphing calculators, computer graphing utilities, spreadsheets, or nongraphing calculators.

INTRODUCTION

One important outcome for this unit is helping students develop an appreciation of the power and limitations of mathematical modeling. They should realize that the two most basic expectations of models are (1) the ability to account for or represent known phenomena and (2) the ability to predict future results. Thus, with the models that students develop in this unit, they should continually be asking such questions as, What will happen if this trend continues? or What if this element is changed?

Other outcomes that we anticipate from this unit are a better understanding of the differences among linear, quadratic, and exponential functions (models) and the patterns of growth that arise from them; a more concrete realization of the vastness of space and the seeming paradox of having very large quantities of debris in orbit yet, at the same time, quite small probabilities of encountering any—although with potentially lethal results should an encounter happen; and an appreciation of the power of mathematics to help us "get our arms around" seemingly unmanageable problems.

Data included in this unit are taken from various NASA sources, but you will want to be alert to updated information and current events related to the problem. For example, three events in early 1996 received extensive coverage in the media. One was the Space Shuttle *Endeavour*'s maneuver to steer clear of a defunct satellite. A second was the breaking loose of a satellite and its 12-mile-long tether during an attempt to deploy it from the Shuttle. A third was the return to Earth of a Chinese satellite, which probably landed somewhere in the Atlantic Ocean. Such events help make more real the concern over the problem of space pollution. Also, you will want to remind your students that such data as the amount of debris in orbit are estimates based on the best technology and information available at a given time. These estimates are continually revised as new information becomes available. You should not be unduly concerned about whether the amount of debris or the rate of accumulation, for example, represents the latest, most precise numbers; rather, you will want to focus on patterns of change and on how those quantities grow or decrease over time under various assumptions, such as linear versus quadratic versus exponential growth. When you find different estimates of some of these quantities, use this excellent opportunity to ask, How shall we adjust our models to account for this new information?

Curriculum Connections:

Functions

Modeling

Statistics

Probability

Geometry

Computing technology provides tools, especially spreadsheets and graphing utilities, that make the study of function concepts and their applications accessible to all students in grades 9–12.

(NCTM 1989, p. 155)

Teaching Standards: *The classroom environment must be one that stimulates discourse, encourages reasoning and sense making, and fosters each student's development of mathematical power.*

Students should have the opportunity to appreciate the persuasiveness of functions through activities such as describing real-world relationships that can be depicted by graphs, reading and interpreting graphs, and sketching graphs of data in which the value of one variable depends on the value of another.

(NCTM 1989, pp. 154–55)

What's out there?

Operating payloads	*5%*
Payloads no longer	
operating	*21%*
Spent stages and gear	*25%*
Breakup debris	*49%*

This computer-generated image shows the thousands of satellites, spent-rocket stages, and breakup debris in low-Earth orbit.

This computer-generated image illustrates Earth's rings formed from human-made orbital debris.

Mathematical Connections:

Interested students can investigate Newton's second law ($F = m \cdot a$) and demonstrate why even a particle of very small mass (m) produces a large force (F) when the acceleration of the particle is great. Remember that acceleration is related to the square of velocity.

GETTING STARTED

In January 1996, two days into their mission, the crew of the Space Shuttle *Endeavour* performed a maneuver to slow its speed by 4 feet per second, thereby steering clear of a 350-pound piece of "space junk," a defunct Air Force satellite that would have passed within 4/5 mile of *Endeavour*. Although the Shuttle was in no danger of collision, NASA flight safety rules call for at least 1.3 miles of separation between the Shuttle and any other orbiting object. The maneuver widened the distance to 6 miles.

The incident, however, called attention to the growing problem of space debris. In seventy-four Shuttle missions, only about six have had to perform maneuvers to avoid orbiting objects; yet the Air Force catalogs nearly 8000 orbiting manufactured objects of grapefruit size and larger. As humans and their vehicles and probes prepare to spend longer and longer times in space, they must also prepare to confront the growing problem of space debris.

NASA scientists are just beginning to realize the enormity of this space-age form of pollution. And just as pollution is creating terrible problems for us on Earth, so, too, are we experiencing hazards with space pollution. Estimates made in 1990 stated that more than 4 million pounds of manufactured materials were in Earth orbit. Of that amount, only 5 percent represented operating payloads; the other 95 percent consisted of human-made debris: old rocket parts, nonfunctioning satellites, discarded tools, the by-products of explosions and collisions, and other odds and ends, as well as countless numbers of smaller objects, such as paint chips and dust-sized particles. On the basis of the rate at which launches were occurring in 1990, we expected the nations in the space business to contribute an additional 1.8 million pounds per year, with an expectation of nearly 2.7 million pounds per year by the year 2000. The prediction warns that if we do not change our ways, we will have 9.5 million pounds of human-made materials circling Earth.

Rings are already forming around Earth—not the rings of rock and dust and ice that encircle other planets, but rings of human-made orbital debris—and their density is increasing. According to Don Kessler, a NASA scientist who has made a career of studying space debris, "Rings are nature's way of saying it doesn't like things in non-circular orbit out of Earth's equatorial plane. Nature wants to tear these objects apart and reform them into either a ring or a single object…it is just a question of when."

The North American Aerospace Defense Command (NORAD) reported in 1986 that 4488 of 6194 radar-trackable objects were orbital debris. The rest included 1582 payloads, 68 interplanetary probes, and 56 items of interplanetary probe debris. A radar-trackable object in space is baseball size or larger, but during hypervelocity, which begins at 3 kilometers per second, particles as small as a paint flake can be damaging or even lethal. By the mid-1980s, ground-based telescopes made it possible for scientists to see marble-sized pieces of orbital debris. From these observations, they concluded that the number of debris objects was many times the number that NORAD had cataloged.

The first loss of a spacecraft part directly attributable to human-made orbital debris occurred during the Shuttle mission of STS-7 in 1983. The crew of the *Challenger* reported an impact crater on one of the orbiter's windows significant enough to require replacement despite the fact that the window was 5/8 inch thick and built to withstand pressures of 8600 pounds per square inch and temperatures up to 482°C. By studying the traces found in the pitted window, NASA determined that the damage was caused by white paint specks about 0.2 millimeter in diameter traveling between 3 and 5 kilometers per second.

Cosmonauts on the Soviet spacecraft *Salyut 7* reported a similar window incident just weeks later and even reported hearing the impact. The *Solar Maximum*

Mission satellite had been in space for fifty months when the crew of STS-41C repaired it in space and returned to Earth with 15 square feet of the insulation blanket and 10 square feet of aluminum louvers showing thousands of pits and excessive wear and tear. The blanket showed thirty-two holes per square foot and the louvers, six holes per square foot, many more than NASA scientists expected; analysis revealed that most of the pits were caused by paint flakes.

Collisions and breakups significantly increase the number of particles orbiting Earth, but they differ in fragmentation and the resulting hazards. Collisions produce smaller fragments and increased hazard. If a 10-pound mass hits a 1000-pound stage at orbital speeds, a tremendous amount of energy is released that could result in 4 million particles and 10 000 larger pieces. Breakups caused by explosions produce fewer small fragments, which gives scientists a greater likelihood that they can learn about the causes of explosions and thus prevent them. For example, when seven second-stage *Delta* rocket breakups occurred three years after launch, scientists were able to determine that they had been caused by unspent hypergolic fuels; this knowledge resulted in launch changes that apparently corrected that problem.

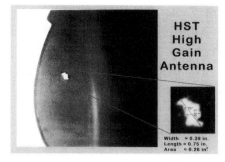

Impact caused by a 1/4-inch particle (happened in orbit)

MODELING SPACE-DEBRIS ACCUMULATION

Space Debris: Is It Really That Bad?

The information presented in this activity includes numbers like 4 million pounds, 1.8 million pounds per year, and 9.5 million pounds. We have become accustomed to reading such numbers, but few of us have an intuitive sense of what they represent. At the beginning of the activity, students are asked to come up with some concrete models of just what such quantities mean. They should find it enjoyable to come up with examples like "9.5 million pounds of pennies would fill …" and other original representations.

Modeling the Problem: Linear Growth

The NASA predictions reported in this activity afford an excellent opportunity to have students create and analyze simple mathematical models. Because mathematicians strive to find the simplest model that will adequately represent the problem, a good starting point for students is to create linear models for the amount of accumulated space debris on the basis of the number of pounds being added each year. In so doing, they will look at the 1990 accumulation rate of 1.8 million pounds per year (rate of increase) and an initial amount of 4 million pounds. If we let the years be represented by t (with $t = 1$ in 1990) and the total pounds of debris by y (in units of 10^6 pounds), our linear model is $y = 1.8t + 4$. Similarly, if we use the rate of 2.7 million pounds per year, we get $y = 2.7t + 4$. This result gives rise to two new questions: (1) Where does the "eventual" 9.5 million pounds come from? and (2) Does either model realistically describe the situation? In this activity, it is also suggested that you make the analogy to velocity. Because students are familiar with distance-rate-time problems, they should be able to see that increasing the amount of debris at a constant rate is equivalent to increasing the distance traveled when moving at a constant speed. Using the two linear equations or a table, students discover that 9.5 million pounds occur in just over three years at the first rate and in just over two years at the second rate (see table 5).

Mathematical Connection: *Students should make the connection between the debris context and the familiar distance-rate-time problems. Both are modeled by linear functions under certain conditions.*

Technology Tip: *Although this investigation can be done manually, it will be of great benefit to have students work with a graphing calculator or a computer graphing package, using either the "trace" feature or a "table" feature. An attempt to locate the 9.5-million-pound value could then be orchestrated by zooming in on the graph or by changing the x-increment in the table to fractions of a year.*

Table 5
Accumulation of Orbital Debris

Year	Amount added (million pounds)	End of year (million pounds)	Amount added (million pounds)	End of year (million pounds)
1990	1.8	5.8	2.7	6.7
1991	1.8	7.6	2.7	9.4
1992	1.8	9.4		

Assessment Tip: *The questions posed in the student pages require students to test conjectures, draw conclusions, and explain and justify their answers.*

A good discussion should result regarding the fact that the prediction did not specify when the 9.5 million pounds would be reached; as students will see later, other factors must be considered when evaluating the prediction. The students should also realize that neither model is accurate because neither rate, 1.8 million pounds per year and 2.7 million pounds per year, applies for the entire period from 1990 through 2000.

Refining the Model: Quadratic Growth

Once students realize that neither of their original attempts at a model truly represents the situation, they should try to adjust the model to account for the fact that neither the rate of 1.8 million pounds per year nor the rate of 2.7 million pounds per year continues throughout the period. Because scientists and mathematicians prefer to start with a simple model and then add complexities to refine it as needed, we make the simplest assumption to account for the changing rate of increase over the period, namely, that the rate of adding debris increases at a constant rate from 1.8 million pounds per year to 2.7 million pounds per year. That is, the rate (velocity) of littering increased by 0.9 million pounds per year achieved in equal increments of 0.09 million pounds per year each year over a ten-year period. The students can then create a table and a graph of the rate of "dumping" versus the year by using the data points (0, 1.8) and (10, 2.7). This *change of rate of dumping* is given by the equation $d = 0.09a + 1.8$, where $a = 0$ in 1990. The increases in both the dumping rate and the total accumulation are shown in table 6 and figure 3.

Curve fitting is a statistical topic that integrates easily into the study of linear and higher-order equations.

(NCTM 1989, p. 168)

Table 6
Rate of Dumping and Total Accumulation

Year	Amount added in year (millions of pounds)	Total in orbit at end of year (millions of pounds)
1990	1.80	5.80
1991	1.89	7.69
1992	1.98	9.67
1993	2.07	11.74
1994	2.16	13.90
1995	2.25	16.15
1996	2.34	18.49
1997	2.43	20.92
1998	2.52	23.44
1999	2.61	26.05
2000	2.70	28.75

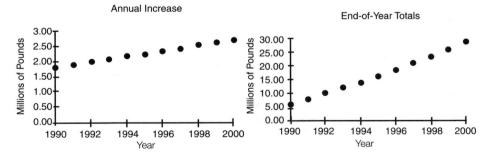

Fig. 3. Graphs showing annual increases and total amounts of debris

At this point emerge a number of important concepts to explore. Although both plots in figure 3, and those that your students generate, may appear to be linear over the ten-year range of the initial data, extending the domain to twenty or thirty or fifty years, as suggested on the student page, makes it evident that the graph of the end-of-year total accumulation is, indeed, not linear. The fact that it is quadratic can be approached from several perspectives:

- Students can manually create a best-fit line and check its predictions against those generated by the table patterns.

- Students can generate linear- and quadratic-regression equations on a graphing calculator and overlay both the linear-regression graph and the quadratic-regression graph on the scatterplot of the data.

- Students can use the method of constant differences and the data from the tables to generate a quadratic equation. This method is summarized in the next section.

Applying the Method of Constant Differences

1. Review the fact that for all linear functions, the differences between successive values of $f(x)$ are constant when x is an integer. We refer to these as "first differences." In the case of quadratic functions, the first differences are not constant, but the differences between them, the "second differences," are constant. This pattern can be extended to higher-order polynomial functions: cubic functions are constant in the third differences, quartic equations are constant in the fourth differences, and so on. Table 7 shows the pattern for the general linear and quadratic cases and for two specific examples from our debris problem.

2. Use the data in table 7 to generate the following equations. Solve them for a, b, and c.

$$a + b + c = 5.8 \qquad\qquad c = 4$$
$$3a + b = 1.89 \qquad\qquad b = 1.755$$
$$2a = 0.09 \qquad\qquad a = 0.045$$

The desired function is $f(x) = 0.045x^2 + 1.755x + 4$, where $f(x)$ gives the amount of debris in orbit at the end of year x and x equals 1 in 1990. Overlay this equation on the earlier scatterplot.

Table 7
Pattern for General Linear and Quadratic Cases with Examples

	Linear function: $f(x) = ax + b$				Quadratic function: $f(x) = ax^2 + bx + c$					
	General Case		$f(x) = 1.8x + 4$			General Case			Debris Example	
$x =$	$f(x)$	First difference	$f(x)$	First difference	$x =$	$f(x)$	First difference	Second difference	$f(x)$	First difference	Second difference
1	$a + b$		5.8		1	$a + b + c$			5.8		
		a		1.8			$3a + b$			1.89	
2	$2a + b$		7.6		2	$4a + 2b + c$		$2a$	7.69		0.09
		a		1.8			$5a + b$			1.98	
3	$3a + b$		9.4		3	$9a + 3b + c$		$2a$	9.67		0.09
		a		1.8			$7a + b$			2.07	
4	$4a + b$		11.2		4	$16a + 4b + c$			11.74		

Velocity-Acceleration Analogy

The student pages compare the quadratic model for debris with the more familiar case of constant acceleration. Students who have studied motion in a physics class should make the connection between examples of uniformly accelerated motion, such as a free fall, a ball rolling down an incline, or a car accelerating at a constant rate, and the "uniform acceleration of space dumping." With your more advanced mathematics students, you will want to pursue the fact that the linear equation $d = 0.09x + 1.8$, where x is the number of years since 1990, is the equation of the tangent to the curve $y = 0.045x^2 + 1.755x + 4$, the equation previously derived. That is, the first equation is the derivative of the second.

Mathematical Connection: *The quadratic model for the buildup of space debris is equivalent to uniformly accelerated motion.*

Curriculum Standards: *The conceptual underpinnings of calculus are recognized and reinforced in this context.*

In this section, students are likely to have the greatest difficulty differentiating among the "rate (velocity) of littering" (e.g., 1.8 million pounds per year in 1990), the "total change in the littering rate over ten years" (i.e., an increase of 0.9 million pounds per year between the 1990 rate of 1.8 million pounds per year and the 2000 rate of 2.7 million pounds per year), and the "rate of change (acceleration) of littering velocity" (an increase of 0.09 million pounds per year each year). You will need to pay special attention to these concepts.

In comparing the quadratic model, $y = 0.045x^2 + 1.755x + 4$, with the two linear models, $y = 1.8x + 4$ and $y = 2.7x + 4$, students will find that the graph of the quadratic lies between the two lines. They should be able to interpret this result in terms of what would happen if the rate of adding debris stayed at 1.8 million pounds per year, was always 2.7 million pounds per year, or gradually changed from 1.8 to 2.7 million pounds per year. They should also determine when the value of the quadratic will surpass the second linear function and recognize that thereafter the quadratic will always produce greater values.

One More Perspective: Exponential Growth

Mathematical Connection: The exponential model is equivalent to compound interest.

The third model proposed in this unit is an exponential one: What will happen if the debris accumulates as a fixed percent of what is already in orbit? This question is, of course, analogous to the familiar problem of compound interest, and it gives an alternative context for exploring the concept of exponential growth. It is a setting in which you will almost surely want students to use a spreadsheet.

The major objective is to help students realize the impact of exponential growth. With a spreadsheet they can hypothesize different rates of increase and explore what would happen if debris were to be added at those rates. The findings can be compared with the patterns of linear and quadratic growth. Some examples are shown in table 8 and the graphs in figure 4; the amounts are in millions of pounds.

Technology makes it possible for students to observe the behavior of many types of functions.

(NCTM 1989, p. 155)

Table 8
Examples of Linear, Quadratic, and Exponential Growth

Number of years	Linear at 1.8(10^6) / year	Linear at 2.7(10^6) / year	Quadratic	Exponential at 20% per year	Exponential at 10% per year
1	5.80	6.70	5.80	4.80	4.40
2	7.60	9.40	7.69	5.76	4.84
3	9.40	12.10	9.67	6.91	5.32
4	11.20	14.80	11.74	8.29	5.86
5	13.00	17.50	13.90	9.95	6.44
10	22.00	31.00	26.05	24.77	10.37
20	40.00	58.00	57.10	153.35	26.91
30	58.00	85.00	97.15	949.51	69.80
50	94.00	139.00	204.25	36 401.75	469.56

Assessment Tip: Students should be expected to give coherent interpretations of what the graphs signify and to use the graphs to predict the behavior of each model for years not shown on the graph.

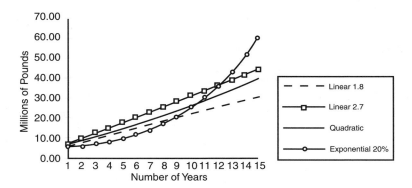

Fig. 4. A comparison of four models

Mission Mathematics: Grades 9–12

What Goes Up Might Come Down: Extending the Models

Students should realize, however, that not everything in orbit stays there forever. Orbiting objects will also be pulled back into Earth's atmosphere, where they will burn up or, on occasion, return to Earth. To be realistic, the models that students develop should take into account both the addition to, and the destruction of, orbital debris.

We do not provide any particular data for this section so that students will have the opportunity to form and test hypotheses of their own. They should try modifications that assume destruction at a fixed rate per year (linear) as well as at a fixed percent (exponential decay). They are looking for models that might predict an eventual decrease in the amount of orbital debris even though we assume that NASA and others will continue to launch payloads and thereby continue to add to the orbital debris. These open-ended investigations are designed to let students experience the search for models that might lead to desirable consequences—although, in reality, we may need to invent the necessary technology to implement the model.

Putting Your Models to Work

Finally, students are encouraged to generate "What if…" questions and to use their models to help generate answers. Before you ask them to formulate their questions, you might want to pose some of your own. The following are examples:

- What if, at the end of 1995, we were able to stop adding to the debris and were able to decrease the existing debris at a rate of 0.35 million pounds per year for the next three years? What would be the total poundage remaining at the end of 1998? What would be the percent of decrease? Note that the answers will vary depending on what assumptions are made about the rate of increase during the years 1990–1995.

- In addition, what if, at the beginning of 1999, new technology would allow us to improve the rate of decrease to 0.65 million pounds per year for a two-year period? What would be the total debris remaining at the end of the century?

MODELING COLLISION EFFECTS

This activity presents a problem of major significance to the aerospace community: the consequences of impact at hypervelocity. Tests done in the NASA laboratories as well as evidence from returned spacecraft confirm the enormous damage that can be rendered by even very small particles striking at orbital speeds.

This activity introduces the concept of *kinetic energy*. If your students are studying physics or physical science, they should be familiar with this form of energy. The unit of a *joule* will be less familiar, since it is a "highbred" unit and not something for which we have everyday references. Rather than dwell on what one joule might be, it is more useful to calculate the kinetic energy of some everyday examples, such as a truck traveling at highway speeds or a hard-hit ball, and then relate other energies, such as the kinetic energy of impact from a paint flake in orbit, as some multiple or fraction of the more familiar examples. You may be surprised to discover that a 1-gram paint chip traveling at orbital speed has nearly 1/10 the kinetic energy of a 3500-pound truck moving at 60 miles per hour and that a 350-pound satellite at orbital speed has 10 000 times the kinetic energy of the truck.

In this section, students must pay close attention to units, and you will want to be sure that they recognize that to be meaningful, their calculations of such quantities as mass, velocity, and energy must be expressed in appropriate units. You will note that the units used in the activity are mixed—pounds, kilograms,

The introduction of new topics and most subsumed objectives should, whenever possible, be embedded in problem situations posed in an environment that encourages students to explore, formulate and test conjectures, prove generalizations, and discuss and apply the results of their investigations.

(NCTM 1989, p. 128)

Assessment Tip: *Students demonstrate their understanding of the concepts through the questions they pose as well as through the answers they give.*

Teaching Tip: Hypervelocity *is defined as 3 kilometers per second or faster. Have your students compare that speed with familiar examples of high speed that they can research or compute, such as the SST airplane, a race car, a "bullet" train, or a hard-hit tennis ball, golf ball, or baseball.*

$$1J = 1\frac{kg \cdot m^2}{s^2}$$

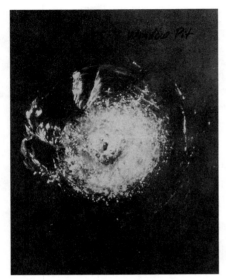

Impact crater on the Space Shuttle Challenger's window created by orbital debris

grams, miles per hour, kilometers per second, and so on—because they are the units commonly used in measuring the associated phenomena. This situation is realistic, and with spreadsheets and calculators, conversions should pose no particular problems. Cautious attention to units, however, is required. Also, some measurements are left for students to find or approximate, such as the mass of a baseball or the velocity at which it may be hit. Sports enthusiasts sometimes carry this sort of information in their heads; others may prefer to use data from their own sports exploits; still others will look up the data in a book of sports statistics.

Again, the purpose of the activity is to foster open-ended investigation and discussion of the relative effects of the linear factor (mass) compared with the quadratic component (velocity). We are less concerned with precise answers to particular questions than we are with the larger concept of how these functions behave.

MODELING COLLISION PROBABILITY

Throughout this unit, we have looked at enormous quantities—millions of pounds—of debris. But we have not yet related those quantities to the vastness of space, even the relatively "close fitting" sphere in which payloads orbit Earth. This activity has students calculate the volume of a "shell" 200 kilometers thick extending from an altitude of 200 to 400 kilometers above Earth—a volume of just over $1.1(10^{11})$ cubic kilometers. If we assume that 4 million pounds (1.8 million kilograms) of debris are evenly distributed throughout this volume, we find the density of debris to be on the order of $1.6(10^{-5})$ kilogram, or 0.016 gram, per cubic kilometer.

In the activity, we assume that the debris has the density of aluminum, 2.7 grams per cubic centimeter. By making this assumption, we can estimate that the 0.016 gram per cubic kilometer represents approximately 0.006 cubic centimeter of debris per cubic kilometer of the shell. The probability of hitting any of that debris is the ratio of the volume of debris to the volume of the shell; hence, we can estimate the probability of hitting the debris to be on the order of $6(10^{-12})$. Removing the simplifying assumption of a 200-kilometer-thick shell does not change the order of magnitude of the probability.

MODELING ORBITAL DEBRIS PROBLEMS

Space Debris: Is It Really That Bad?

One problem with which NASA and space scientists from other countries must deal is the accumulation of space debris in orbit around Earth. Such debris includes payloads that are no longer operating; spent stages of rockets; assorted parts and lost tools; debris from the breakup of larger objects or from collisions between objects; and countless small pieces, such as flakes of paint and even smaller objects. Because bodies in Earth orbit travel at approximately 17 500 miles per hour, a collision with even a tiny object can have catastrophic effects. In 1990, scientists estimated that a total of 4 million pounds of debris was in Earth orbit. They also estimated that at that time, we were adding 1.8 million pounds per year to the already serious problem, which in a few years would result in 9.5 million pounds of orbital debris. The 1990 prediction also stated that the amount of debris being added per year was anticipated to increase to a rate of 2.7 million pounds per year by the year 2000.

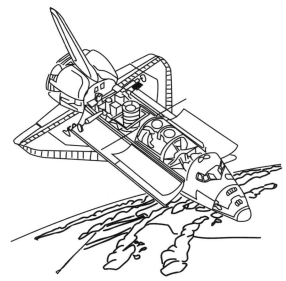

◆ How much is 4 million pounds of anything? Or 9.5 million? Give at least three concrete examples that would help another person get a sense of how much *millions of pounds* of debris is. For example, finish the following sentence.

A total of 9.5 million pounds of pennies would fill_____.

Modeling the Problem: Linear Growth

The problem of determining the amount of debris in space and the anticipated rate of increase of such matter is not one that can be solved directly. We cannot locate, count, and weigh all the objects in orbit. Nor can we predict with assurance when two of them will collide. Instead, we must rely on mathematical models to help us represent the problem and identify trends and expected outcomes. In these activities, you will create and compare various mathematical models to help you investigate some of the questions raised by the proliferation of orbital debris. These models are greatly simplified in their assumptions so that you can investigate them with calculators, spreadsheets, and graphing utilities, but they provide insight into the process of mathematical modeling and its importance.

When creating models, mathematicians favor the simplest model that will account for the phenomena in question. Generally, a linear model gives the simplest case. So, using the reported 1990 rate of increase of 1.8 million pounds per year and assuming 4 million pounds of existing debris at the beginning of 1990, write a linear model to predict the number of pounds of orbital debris at the end of any given year, t. Assume that $t = 1$ represents 1990.

Write a second linear model using the predicted 2.7 million-pounds-per-year rate of increase and the initial 4 million pounds for 1990.

```

```

Evaluate each model for several years to determine the year in which the predicted 9.5 million pounds of accumulated debris would occur:

With the first model:_____

With the second model: _____

◆ When a vehicle travels at a constant rate, r, for a length of time, t, the distance traveled by the vehicle is modeled by a linear function. Compare the familiar linear model for distance-rate-time with your linear models for accumulating space debris. Why can we refer to your linear models as "constant-velocity models for amassing space debris"?

◆ Do you think that either of your linear models accurately represents the situation of escalating amounts of space debris as described in the original paragraph? Why or why not?

Refining the Model: Quadratic Growth

Does either rate, 1.8 million pounds per year or 2.7 million pounds per year, tell us how much debris is building up between 1990 and 2000? Which rate of increase should we use? Obviously the amount being added each year is changing during this period, but by how much each year? The problem is one of acceleration, not constant velocity, so we need to adjust our model.

Again, let's make the simplest assumption: the rate at which we are adding

debris increases at a constant rate from 1.8 million pounds per year in 1990 to 2.7 million pounds per year in 2000. This change means that over the ten-year period from the end of 1990 through 2000, the rate (velocity) of littering will increase by 0.9 million pounds per year (2.7 − 1.8 = 0.9), and we are making the assumption that this increase is achieved in equal annual increments of 0.09 million pounds per year in each year of the decade. Complete the following table to show the amount of debris added each year and the total amount in orbit at the end of the year.

Year	Amount Added in Year (millions of pounds)	Total in Orbit at End of Year (millions of pounds)
1990	1.8	5.8
1991		
1992		
1993		
1994		
1995		
1996		
1997		
1998		
1999		
2000	2.7	

Since we assumed that the increase in the velocity of littering was achieved in equal annual increments, you can write a linear equation that describes the increase in the amount of debris being added each year (i.e., the increase in the annual velocity of littering) as a function of the number of years since 1990. In this case, we let $a = 0$ in 1990 because we are assuming that the 1990 rate of 1.8 million pounds per year is our baseline rate. Then $d = f(a)$ represents the rate of littering a years after 1990.

```

```

◆ The situation described in your equation, where the rate of increase of litter is itself increasing at a constant rate, is analogous to a vehicle that accelerates at a constant rate from an initial velocity, v_0, to a final velocity, v_f. Use the data generated in the foregoing table to create a scatterplot of the total number of pounds of orbital debris that have accumulated relative to the year. Your graph should cover the period from 1990 through 2000.

◆ Fit a line to your data and decide whether the accumulation of debris appears to be linear. Write your conclusion and describe the evidence on which you based your decision.

◆ Using a graphing calculator or a computer graphing program, calculate the linear-regression equation for these data. Do your calculations support a linear relationship? Explain. How does this line compare with the line that you fitted manually?

◆ Next generate a quadratic-regression equation for the same data. Write the quadratic-regression model here:

How well does this equation fit the data compared with the linear approximation?

◆ Compare your quadratic-regression equation with the two linear-regression equations that you developed earlier. In each case, use your models to predict the accumulation of debris after twenty years, thirty years, and fifty years. Describe the behavior of the linear model versus the quadratic model over time.

◆ For the period from 1990 to 2000, the graph of the quadratic model lies between the graphs of the two linear models. Explain why this result is reasonable. Will the quadratic graph always lie between the two linear graphs? Explain.

◆ Explain why the quadratic model for the debris problem can be described as a "uniform acceleration" model.

One More Perspective: Exponential Growth

So far, you have looked at two models, a "constant velocity" linear model and a "uniformly accelerated" quadratic model. Let's look at one more model.

Suppose that the amount of litter added each year grew not by a fixed number of pounds but by a fixed percent of the amount already in space—a situation analogous to an investment of money with interest compounded annually. For example, what would happen to the original 4 million pounds if the litter added each year was 20 percent of the amount already in orbit? Complete the following table to determine the amount of debris that would accumulate over the period from 1990 to 2000. A spreadsheet is recommended for this activity.

Year	Amount Added Each Year Equaling 20% of Previous Amount (millions of pounds)	Total in Orbit at End of Year (millions of pounds)
(1989)	(N/A)	4
1990	0.8	4.8
1991	0.96	
1992		
1993		
1994		
1995		
1996		
1997		
1998		
1999		
2000		

Write an exponential model to describe the growth of the original 4 million pounds of debris over the years:

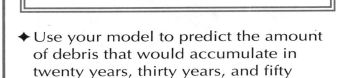

✦ Use your model to predict the amount of debris that would accumulate in twenty years, thirty years, and fifty years.

✦ Economists use what is referred to as the "rule of 72" to predict how long it will take an amount of money to double if it is invested at a rate of R percent compounded annually. According to the rule of 72, the doubling time, D, is given by the equation

$$D = 72/R.$$

Use the rule of 72 to predict how long it will take for the amount of debris to double if littering compounds at the rate of 20 percent per year. How long will it take for the original 4 million pounds to increase to 32 million pounds? Do the data in your table agree with those calculations?

✦ If the growth of space debris was following an exponential model and concern arose that it would take only twelve years to double the amount of space debris, what must the annual percent increase in debris have been to result in this doubling time of twelve years?

What Goes Up Might Come Down: Extending the Models

All the models you have developed thus far assume that the additional debris added each year stays in orbit and accumulates there. But, in fact, every year some of the debris slows down enough to re-enter the atmosphere where it burns up or, on rare occasions, returns to Earth. Assume for the moment that 10 percent of the debris in orbit at the beginning of any year will be destroyed during that year. Modify your linear, quadratic, and exponential models to account for the situation in which additional debris is being added each year while 10 percent of what was already in orbit is being destroyed.

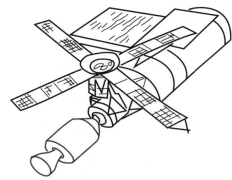

✦ In which case—linear, quadratic, or exponential—does the assumption of a 10 percent re-entry rate have the greatest effect?

✦ Assume the same rates of adding debris as you did when you generated the models, but try different rates of annual destruction of orbital debris. In each situation, does a destruction rate exist that will result in a net decrease in orbital debris despite the fact that additional debris is being added? What might be some advantages of knowing if such a rate is possible?

Putting Your Models to Work

The power of mathematical models comes from their ability to enable us to ask "What if?" questions. An earlier question is an example: What if we could increase the rate at which orbital debris is destroyed? Other questions might include these: What if we decrease the rate at which we are adding debris? What if we decrease the rate at which we are adding debris *and* find a way to increase the rate at which existing debris is destroyed? Such questions lead to open-ended investigations using mathematical models.

◆ Working with a partner or a small group, generate two or three specific questions that you would like to investigate.

1. What if

2. What if

3. What if

Describe a plan for investigating your questions using spreadsheets, graphing utilities, or other appropriate technology.

Attach copies of your data with commentary that describes what the data represent and what you conclude from your investigation.

Using your models and the information they generated, prepare a written or oral presentation that helps your audience think about steps we might take in an attempt to manage the problem of orbital debris and the likely consequences of not doing so.

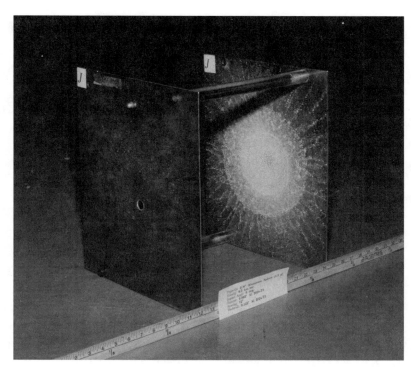

A test of the Whipple bumper, showing damage. The projectile used to test this concept is a small aluminum ball. The function of the bumper is to break up the projectile, disperse the fragments, and reduce their velocity below that of the original projectile, thereby eliminating the projectile's ability to penetrate a second layer.

MODELING COLLISION EFFECTS

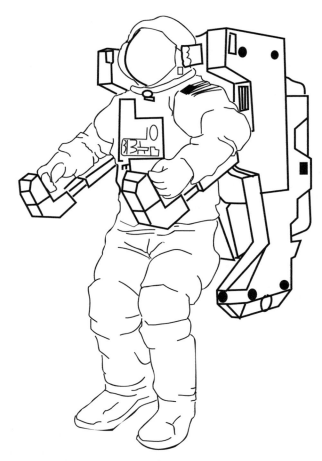

An "inventory" published in 1986 by the North American Aerospace Defense Command (NORAD) and NASA's Goddard Space Flight Center identified 6194 radar-trackable objects, that is, of baseball size and larger, in space. In addition, NASA experts estimated the presence of 30 000 marble- to baseball-sized objects, trillions of tiny paint flakes, and tens to hundreds of trillions of dust-sized particles of aluminum oxide. When objects, even the very small ones, travel at *hypervelocity* (defined to be in excess of 3 kilometers per second), the effects of a collision can be devastating. For example, an orbiting particle 0.3 millimeter in diameter, just slightly larger than a grain of salt, can puncture a spacesuit with a hole large enough to force an astronaut to return quickly to the spacecraft or risk depressurization.

An object in motion possesses kinetic energy, from the Greek word *kinetos,* meaning *moving.* Physicists have determined that the kinetic energy (*KE*) of a body of mass *m* traveling with a velocity *v* is given by the relationship $KE = (1/2)mv^2$. Kinetic energy is measured in units that may not be immediately familiar, so we attempt to minimize confusion by using metric units consistently in the following activity. In this system, if mass is measured in kilograms (kg) and velocity is measured in meters per second (m/s), energy will be measured in units called *joules* (J) where

$$1J = 1\frac{kg \cdot m^2}{s^2}.$$

◆ To get a better sense of what one joule of energy means, calculate the kinetic energy of a 3500-pound truck traveling at 60 miles per hour. Compare that result with the kinetic energy of a 350-pound satellite orbiting at 17 500

miles per hour and with the energy of a 1-gram paint chip orbiting at the same speed. Remember that 1 mile = 1.61 kilometer, 1 kilometer = 0.62 mile, 1 pound = 0.45 kilogram, and 1 kilogram = 2.20 pounds.

◆ What might be the kinetic energy of a hard-hit baseball or a well-served tennis ball?

NASA studies the effects of high-velocity collisions in its Hypervelocity Impact Test Facility (HITF) at the Johnson Space Center in Houston. The HITF contains three light-gas "guns." These guns accelerate particles that range in diameter from 100 microns (0.1 mm) to 10 millimeters at velocities in the range of 2 km/s to 7 km/s; the high-speed particles are fired into samples of various materials in different configurations to study the effects of the impacts. Each gun fires particles of different masses: gun A, 0.0015 milligram to 5.8 milligrams; gun B, 0.091 milligram to 46 milligrams; and gun C, 46 milligrams to 1.45 grams.

The highest velocities achieved in the laboratory, about 7 km/s, correspond to speeds of nearly 16 000 miles per hour; nevertheless, NASA estimates that only about 25 percent of the orbital-debris impacts occur at speeds of 8 km/s or less. Thus, it is necessary to rely on mathematical modeling to scale the experimental results observed in the laboratory to higher velocities.

Using a computer spreadsheet or the table function of your graphing calculator, create a model that allows you to calculate the kinetic energies of various objects, from microscopic particles moving at orbital or near-orbital speeds to familiar objects moving at realistic Earth-bound speeds.

◆ What effect does mass have on the kinetic energy of a moving body? For example, if two objects, one with ten times the mass of the other, travel at the same speed, how do their kinetic energies compare?

◆ What effect does velocity have on the kinetic energy of a moving body? For example, if two objects of equal mass are moving, one with ten times the velocity of the other, how do their kinetic energies compare?

◆ Which factor, mass or velocity, makes the greater contribution to the total amount of kinetic energy? Why?

◆ NASA scientists have stated that trackable objects pose a relatively small hazard to spacecraft but that the vast number of smaller breakup-debris particles present a hazard disproportionate to their size. Why do you suppose that they would say that?

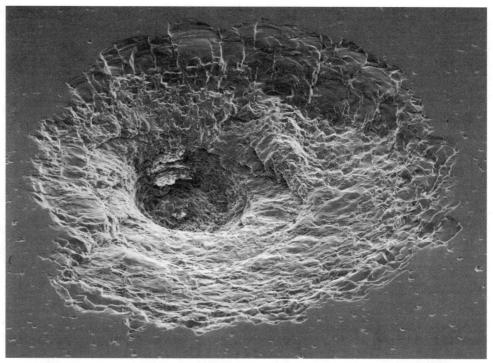

A scanning electron micrograph of a tiny crater in a window on the Space Shuttle Challenger in June 1983

MODELING COLLISION PROBABILITY

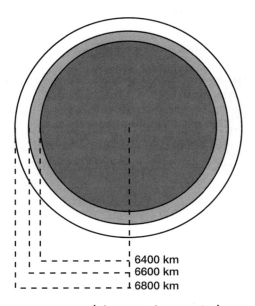

6400 km
6600 km
6800 km

Most manned spacecraft orbit at about 100 to 200 miles (or 160 to 320 kilometers) above Earth. How likely is it that such an orbiting vehicle will encounter a particle of orbital debris? We can use a geometrical model to estimate collision probabilities.

Consider this cross section of Earth. Earth's radius is about 6400 kilometers. Even though the figure is not constructed to scale, it should be apparent that the region in which spacecraft orbit is very close to Earth as astronomical distances go.

Next, envision a series of spherical "shells" surrounding Earth. The first includes the atmosphere and is below the surrounding sphere of orbital flight. As a first approximation, made to simplify the calculations, we can let each shell be 200 kilometers in thickness. Thus we are interested in the shell that lies between the two spheres of radius 6600 kilometers and 6800 kilometers. What is the volume of that shell?

Suppose that the 4 million pounds of orbital debris described earlier are randomly distributed within this shell. If that debris has the density of aluminum (2.7 grams per cubic centimeter), how much debris would you expect to encounter in each cubic kilometer of space? Use the models that you developed earlier to study how the probability of encountering space debris changes as the total amount of debris escalates. If you remove our simplifying assumption and let the "shell of orbital flight" be from 160 to 320 kilometers, as stated in the opening paragraph, will your conclusions change appreciably? In other words, are we justified in making the simplifying assumptions? Prepare a written or oral report of your findings.

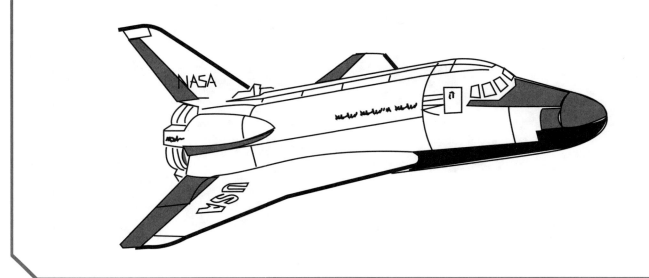

FINDING OUR WAY

Mission Mathematics

Linking Aerospace and the NCTM Standards

A NASA/NCTM Project

Travelers are always interested in knowing where they are at any point in a journey. Early explorers navigated the seas to find out about their world. The technology of the day helped them know their approximate location and reach their destinations. For example, the magnetic compass gave sailors directional headings. The quadrant allowed sailors to measure the altitude of the Pole Star, thus helping them determine the latitude of their ship. The astrolabe and the Jacob's staff were other devices used to determine latitude. The sextant was invented as a means to help find the longitude of a ship at sea.

The cumulative information about sailing the seas was published as tables that all sea captains could use. An American, Nathaniel Bowditch (1773–1838), played an important role in developing these navigational tables. Bowditch used his mathematical knowledge to correct the tables commonly used in the 1700s. His corrections were remarkably accurate. In fact, a prospective sea captain enrolled in a navigational course today will likely use a copy of Bowditch's tables.

Early aviators employed visual landmarks to navigate in the air just as early sailors used them at sea. Since airplanes were faster than ships, sextants and astrolabes were not appropriate tools. Pilots could not sight and compute fast enough to make accurate estimates of location. A need arose for faster calculations relative to position. Radio techniques filled this need and signaled the beginning of a new era in navigation. The new technologies developed for air travel were adopted by sailors.

Advanced aviation and space travel heightened the importance of fast and accurate navigation. The need for this technology was acutely felt by the Department of Defense. The security of the nation depended on our ability to position our military assets accurately and to determine the exact location of the military units of other countries. NASA's efforts in the development of satellites led to the creation of a national system for navigation. The Global Positioning System (GPS) is a constellation of twenty-four satellites put into orbit by the Department of Defense. By "locking on" to the radio signals transmitted from at least three satellites, a process known as triangulation, a GPS receiver can provide navigation information to anyone anywhere in the world in any weather condition.

Advanced hand-held units use a five-parallel-channel receiver. Three channels lock on to satellites for triangulating position. A fourth channel locks on for three-dimensional navigation, which includes altitude. These four channels continuously and simultaneously track the four satellites in the best geometrical position relative to the receiver. The fifth channel tracks all other visible satellites, allowing the receiver to switch quickly to alternative satellites in the event that one of the four primary satellites becomes obstructed. Thus, in adverse conditions, such as in valleys or dense woods, a user can depend on continuous and uninterrupted accurate navigation.

These hand-held units can be purchased at sporting-equipment outlets. Anglers use them to record favorite fishing spots so they can return another day. Hunters use them to find locations where game has been sighted. It probably will not be long before golfing enthusiasts will devise a way to determine accurately the length of their golf shots using GPS. Under discussion is the installation of GPS systems in cars and trucks to help drivers navigate the highway systems. This immensely powerful technology related to navigation has become available to everyone and will be used in many creative ways in our changing world.

MATHEMATICS AND APPLICATIONS OF A GLOBAL POSITIONING SYSTEM

A Global Positioning System (GPS) is a space-based, time-of-arrival radio-positioning system that provides twenty-four-hour, three-dimensional position, velocity, and time information to suitably equipped users anywhere on or near Earth's surface. On 26 June 1993, the U.S. Department of Defense set into Earth's orbit the last of twenty-four satellites that together make up NAVSTAR (**Nav**igation **S**atellite **T**iming **a**nd **R**anging), a GPS that was conceived in the 1970s to provide its users with nothing short of a quantum leap as a utility for navigation and positioning. With appropriate technology—equipment that is decreasing in price yet growing in features, sophistication, and availability—GPS users can accurately pinpoint their positions virtually anywhere on Earth.

PURPOSES

This unit presents the mathematics that underlies the GPS. It develops a conceptualization of GPS through examples in one, two, and three dimensions; identifies the mathematics inherent in the systems; and offers a series of activities together with comments and solutions to accompany the student pages.

INTRODUCTION

A GPS is defined by three components. The first is the *space segment.* NAVSTAR consists of twenty-four satellites, called the operational constellation. Twenty-one navigation satellites and three active spares circle Earth in twelve-hour orbits. The orbits repeat the same ground track once each day, and the orbit altitude is such that each satellite repeats the same track and configuration approximately each twenty-four hours. This operational constellation provides GPS users with five to eight satellites visible from any point on Earth.

The *control segment* is the second component of a GPS. It consists of a system of tracking stations throughout the world. The system monitors satellite signals, from which it creates orbital models for those satellites. The models compute precise orbital data, known as ephemeris, as well as clock corrections for each satellite. A master control station in Colorado sends ephemeris and clock data to the satellites, which then relay some of that information by means of a radio signal to GPS receivers, part of the third segment of a GPS known as the user segment.

The *user segment* is made up of the GPS receivers and their users. GPS receivers convert satellite signals into position, velocity, and time estimates. Data from four satellites are required to compute the earthly dimensions of position (latitude, longitude, altitude) and time.

Student page 52 shows the essential elements of a GPS. The mathematics on which we concentrate is that used in the triangulation process. *Triangulation* refers to the determination of an unknown position using distances from one or more known positions. In a three-dimensional GPS, we know the positions of the satellites that send radio signals picked up by a GPS receiver. Because radio signals travel at a constant speed, we can determine how far away we are from each satellite by knowing the travel time for each signal.

Errors, however, creep into the system from several sources. We may inaccurately calculate a radio signal's travel time, depending on the synchronization of a satellite's clock with the one in the receiver. As illustrated on student page 52, because the radio signal is traveling in Earth's atmosphere—not in a vacuum—the speed of the radio wave may not be constant. At a signal speed of about 186 000 miles per second, even a slight change can drastically alter the determination of the GPS receiver position.

Curriculum Connections:

Geometry

Algebra

A hand-held GPS receiver

The union of GPS with state-of-the-art mapping techniques may help us to locate, manage, and enjoy Earth's resources better and to navigate more precisely on and above Earth. Smart-vehicle location and navigation systems will help travelers avoid busy freeways by locating more efficient travel routes. Travel by air and sea will be safer in all weather conditions. Commercial and public enterprises with significant mobile resources, such as utilities, bus lines, and package-delivery fleets, will be more efficient and effective in resource management.

It is the intent of this standard that, whenever possible, real-world situations will provide a context for both introducing and applying geometric topics.

(NCTM 1989, p. 157)

Teaching Tip: *Because discussions of navigation and positioning systems can cut across grade levels and mathematics courses, we begin with a one-dimensional example. You will need to determine the entry point at which you and your students can most comfortably begin the development as well as the level of mathematics you intend to draw on in working through and extending the ideas. The activities can be done with informal, visual techniques or through a more advanced analytical approach.*

Related *Mission Mathematics* **Activities:** *See the unit "Advanced Communication Systems" for a consideration of the mathematics involved in transmitting signals through space.*

In the development that follows, the intent is to help students conceptualize two essential components of the triangulation process: (1) using signal travel time to determine distance and (2) dealing with errors inherent in a positioning system. The development begins with examples of sound waves traveling in one and two dimensions, drawn from familiar settings. The examples are intended to help students explore the mathematics of time-of-arrival positioning in systems less complex than the three dimensions of GPS.

GETTING STARTED

Use student page 52 to introduce the components of a three-dimensional GPS. Discuss the meaning of triangulation and ask students for examples of triangulation that they might know about in their lives. Talk about the speed of light and the speed of sound, which are numerical constants that will be needed for calculations in many of the GPS activities. Give students an overview of the activities that you intend to carry out in class, including the development of one-, two-, and three-dimensional cases.

DETERMINING POSITION IN ONE DIMENSION

Introduce the one-dimensional setting described on student page 53: locating a football coach somewhere along the sideline of a football field (fig. 5). Help students identify the three calculations required in a time-of-arrival positioning system such as a GPS.

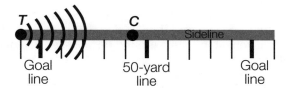

Fig. 5. A coach on a football-field sideline

1. *Determine the travel time of a signal from a transmitter in a known position to a receiver in an unknown position:* In the one-dimensional activities, a coach is moving along the sideline of a football field. Positioned at one or both ends of the field are sound-wave transmitters, and the coach wears a special receiver designed to record the time of arrival of a sound wave. Two elements of the system are required for us to determine the travel time of the signal from the transmitter to the receiver:

   • The signal transmitter must maintain a clock that is highly accurate. Each satellite of the NAVSTAR GPS has four atomic clocks, each accurate to within a billionth of a second a year.

   • We must have some way of knowing when each broadcast is made from the transmitter. In the one-dimensional scenario, we assume that a sound is broadcast every minute on the minute. By comparing the time of arrival with a known transmission time, we can determine the travel time of the signal. In the NAVSTAR GPS, each radio signal contains a code that identifies the time of the signal's transmission from the satellite. A GPS receiver decodes the signal and compares the time of transmission with the time of reception.

2. *Determine the distance traveled by a signal:* In the one-dimensional activities, we assume that sound travels at 1100 feet per second. Knowing the travel time and the travel rate, we can calculate distance using the familiar relationship distance = rate x time. (Later we consider radio waves traveling at 186 000 miles per second sent from orbiting satellites.)

3. *Determine the position of the receiver:* In one dimension, if we know the position of the signal transmitter and the distance traveled by the signal, we

can add or subtract along a straight line to identify the receiver's position. Inherent in the position determination is the use of a coordinate system within which we can carry out that calculation. The culminating activity in the development of a one-dimensional time-of-arrival positioning system is describing the system using a conventional number line rather than a football-field sideline (see student page 54, exercise 9).

Solutions:

Student page 53 illustrates the calculations associated with time-of-arrival positioning.

1. It will take 0.1636 second. The distance from T to C is 60 yards, or 180 feet, so using $d = r \cdot t$, we find that $t = 180$ ft $\div$ 1100 ft/sec = 0.1636 sec.

2. C is just outside the 40-yard line closer to T (d = 1100 ft/sec $\cdot$ 0.14 sec = 154 ft = 51.3 yds).

3. If C is on the 30-yard line nearer to T, C is 40 yards, or 120 feet, from T. Using the technique shown in question 1 yields t = 0.1091 sec. If C is on the 30-yard line farther from T, C is 80 yards, or 240 feet, from T, so t = 0.2182 sec.

4. If C is at the goal line closer to T, d = 10 yds and t = 0.0273 sec. If C is at the other goal line, d = 110 yds and t = 0.3000 sec. The difference is 0.2727 second. (Another way to approach this problem is to recognize that the goal lines are 100 yards, or 300 feet, apart, and it takes t = 300 ft $\div$ 1100 ft/sec = 0.2727 sec for a sound wave to travel that distance.)

5. (a) The elapsed time is 0.0762 second and d = 83.8200 ft = 27.9400 yds. C is just inside the 18-yard line closer to T. (b) The elapsed time is 0.1238 second and d = 136.1800 ft = 45.3933 yds. C is between the 35- and 36-yard lines closer to T. (c) If C is at the 12-yard line farther from T, d = 98 yds and t = 0.2673 sec. The receiver clock reads 0:57:00.2673.

Clock Error

Under ideal conditions, only one transmitter would be required in a one-dimensional system. A user would determine the transmission time for a signal, use that time to calculate the distance traveled by the signal, and then move that distance from the known position of the transmitter to identify the position of the receiver. Under such ideal conditions, it is also necessary to make assumptions about the general position of the receiver, since a signal broadcast from a single point on a line could identify a receiver on either side of the transmitter. In the football-field scenario, the coach is along the playing-field sideline, not along the part of the line that extends beyond the end zone of the field.

But conditions are seldom ideal in applications of a time-of-arrival positioning system such as a GPS. The clock error introduced in the one-dimensional positioning activities (student page 54) represents one of several errors that typically occur in a GPS: the receiver clock is not precisely synchronized with the transmitter clock. In this realistic situation, a second transmitter at the opposite end of the sideline, together with the constant and known information within the system, is required to fix the position of the receiver accurately:

(a) The distance between T_1 and T_2 is 360 feet. Regardless of the location of the coach at any point between the two transmitters, the sum of the transmission times for the signals must be t = 360 ft $\div$ 1100 ft/sec = 0.3273 sec.

(b) Because the clock error is in the receiver, it is constant regardless of the source of the signal. Let e represent this constant error.

In the example given (see question 6 on student page 54), the coach's receiver runs 0.01 second fast; thus, the calculated transmission times from the two

Mathematical Connection: *Along with the challenge of describing a positioning system with a conventional number line rather than a football-field sideline, students, as they complete these activities, will begin to connect with the mathematics that underlies the process of triangulation that is used in time-of-arrival positioning.*

transmitters are incorrect. Call these erroneous times t_1 and t_2. They are related to the actual transmission times, T_1 and T_2, respectively, as follows:

$$T_1 = t_1 - e$$

and

$$T_2 = t_2 - e.$$

We can use these equations and the information in (a) to determine the following relationships:

$$T_1 + T_2 = \left(t_1 - e\right) + \left(t_2 - e\right) = 0.3273$$
$$t_1 + t_2 - 2e = 0.3273$$
$$e = \frac{1}{2}\left(t_1 + t_2 - 0.3273\right)$$

These relationships furnish sufficient information to determine d_1, the distance from T_1 to the receiver at C:

$$d_1 = \left(t_1 - e\right) \cdot 1100$$
$$= \left[t_1 - \frac{1}{2}\left(t_1 + t_2 - 0.3273\right)\right] \cdot 1100$$
$$= \frac{1}{2}\left(1100\right)\left(t_1 - t_2 + 0.3273\right)$$
$$= 550\left(t_1 - t_2 + 0.3273\right)$$

In a similar manner, $d_2 = 550(t_2 - t_1 + 0.3273$.

Solutions:

Student page 54 affords an opportunity to carry out additional calculations in time-of-arrival positioning where clock error is a factor.

7. (a) The receiver clock generates a positioning error of 10 yards, or 30 feet, which is equivalent to a clock error of 30 ft ÷ 1100 ft/sec = 0.0273 sec. The receiver clock is running 0.0273 second fast. (b) The transmitter at T_2 is 70 yards, or 210 feet, from C. Sound requires 210 ft ÷ 1100 ft/sec = 0.1909 sec to travel that distance. Using the clock error determined in (a), we find that the receiver clock will read 1:27:00.2182.

8. Use the relationship $d_1 = 550(t_1 - t_2 + 0.3273)$ to determine the distance in feet from T_1 to C. We can also use $d_2 = 550(t_2 - t_1 + 0.3273)$ to determine the distance from T_2 to C. We have $t_1 = 0.0892$ sec and $t_2 = 0.2981$ sec. Therefore,

$$d_1 = 550(0.0892 - 0.2981 + 0.3273)$$
$$= 65.12 \text{ ft}$$
$$= 21.7067 \text{ yd}$$

and

$$d_2 = 550(0.2981 - 0.0892 + 0.3273)$$
$$= 294.91 \text{ ft}$$
$$= 98.3033 \text{ yd.}$$

This shows that C is between the 11- and 12-yard lines closer to T_1. Note that d_1 and d_2 sum to 120 yards.

Several ways are available to justify that the clocks are not synchronized. One way is to compare the sum of the two transmission times, t_1 and t_2, with the time required for a sound wave to travel from T_1 to T_2. Here, $t_1 + t_2 = 0.3873$ sec, yet earlier we determined that sound travels from T_1 to T_2 in 0.3273 second. Because these values differ, we can conclude that the clocks are not synchronized. Another way to justify that the clocks are not synchronized is to compare the position of C determined from each transmission. Using t_1 in the $d = r \cdot t$ equation, we know that C is 32.7 yards from T_1, between the 22- and 23-yard lines closer to T_1; using t_2, we know that C is 109.3 yards from T_2, between the goal line and the 1-yard line closer to T_1. These are not the same position fix.

To determine the clock error, we can use the relationship

$$e = \frac{1}{2}\left(t_1 + t_2 - 0.3273\right)$$
$$= \frac{1}{2}\left(0.0892 + 0.2981 - 0.3273\right)$$
$$= 0.0300.$$

The receiver clock runs 0.03 second fast. (How do we know whether the clock is running slow or fast?)

9. The generalization is similar to the foregoing situations, except that the distance between X_1 and X_2 is fixed but unknown. When fixed on a number line, that distance is $|x_1 - x_2|$ and the time required for a sound wave to travel that distance is $t = (|x_1 - x_2|$ ft $\div$ 1100 ft/sec) seconds. The receiver-clock error is

$$e = \frac{1}{2}\left(t_1 + t_2 - |x_1 - x_2| \text{ft} \div 1100 \text{ ft/sec}\right)$$
$$= \frac{1}{2}\left(t_1 + t_2\right) - \frac{1}{2200}|x_1 - x_2| \text{ sec.}$$

The distance from x_1 to P is

$$d_1 = 550\left(t_1 - t_2 + |x_1 - x_2| \text{ft} \div 1100 \text{ ft/sec}\right)$$
$$= 550\left(t_1 - t_2\right) + \frac{1}{2}|x_1 - x_2| \text{ ft.}$$

In a similar manner, we have

$$d_2 = 550\left(t_2 - t_1\right) + \frac{1}{2}|x_1 - x_2| \text{ ft.}$$

DETERMINING POSITION IN TWO DIMENSIONS

Activities in this set extend students' conceptualization of time-of-arrival positioning. The setting is a two-dimensional system situated on Lake Superior in the north-central United States. A ship has left the harbor at Duluth, Minnesota, and uses time-of-arrival positioning to track its progress across Lake Superior. Sound waves are again used as the signal, broadcast from foghorns on the lake and received by the ship's navigator (fig. 6).

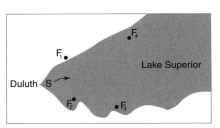

Fig. 6. Locations of ship and foghorns

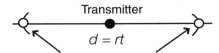

Transmitter

$$d = rt$$

Fig. 7. Two possible position fixes in a one-dimensional system

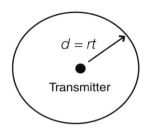

$$d = rt$$

Transmitter

Fig. 8. An infinite number of possible position fixes in a two-dimensional system

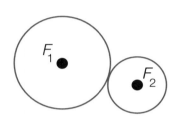

F_1 F_2

Fig. 9. Transmission broadcast circles are tangent: one possible position fix

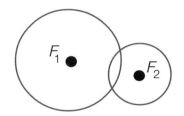

F_1 F_2

Fig. 10. Transmission broadcast circles intersect: two possible position fixes

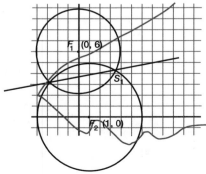

F_1 (0, 6)

S

F_2 (1, 0)

Fig. 11. Broadcast circles for F_1 and F_2

We begin exploring the two-dimensional positioning problem under ideal circumstances wherein no clock error is inherent in the system. By using travel times for sound waves broadcast from foghorns at fixed locations, the ship's navigator can determine broadcast ranges from one or more foghorns. On a two-dimensional level, each broadcast range defines a circle whose center is a foghorn, and the navigator must consider intersections of two or more circles to pinpoint the ship's location.

It is again necessary to make assumptions about the general position of the receiver. Transmissions broadcast from two points (here, the foghorns) on a plane often result in two potential locations for a ship—the two points of intersection of the two circles emanating from the foghorns. Some knowledge of the ship's point of departure, or at least its general path across the lake, must be assumed to allow us to choose correctly from the two possible ship locations. Without knowledge at hand to make such assumptions, we need time-of-arrival data from three foghorns to rule out an erroneous position fix.

The activities of two-dimensional positioning conclude with a consideration of clock error and a summary of two-dimensional time-of-arrival positioning. When the receiver clock is not synchronized with the transmission clocks, the ship's navigator must deal with a constant but unknown clock error. In two dimensions, this translates into foghorn signal ranges that are a constant distance beyond or inside the true signal ranges. One approach to determining position and clock error is presented here.

Conceptualizing the System

Use student page 55 and the open-ended question 1 to discuss with students the components of a two-dimensional time-of-arrival positioning system. Compare the components of the two-dimensional positioning system with those of the one-dimensional system:

- Both use transmitters and receivers to determine sound-wave travel time.

- Both use the relationship distance = rate • time to determine how far a sound wave has traveled.

- Instead of identifying two possible position fixes, as in the one-dimensional system (fig. 7), a two-dimensional system has an infinite number of possible position fixes from one signal, represented by a circle (fig. 8).

- Accurate information from two transmitters can be used to fix at most two possible positions. Additional information—for example, a ship's existing course or information from additional signals—is needed to fix one true position (figs. 9 and 10).

- Because of the possibility of receiver-clock error, information from no fewer than three transmitters is required for an accurate position fix (see the diagram on student page 57).

A Closer Look

Ask students to determine how the foghorn distances and the ship's positions shown in the grid and table on student page 55 might have been calculated and have them verify the information. For example, to verify that the first recorded signal from F_1 is 4 miles from the ship, use the distance equation and the reception time indicated for record 1:

19.2000 sec • 1 100 ft/sec = 21 120 ft = 4 mi from F_1

One way to locate the ship is to determine the equations for the transmission-broadcast circles from two foghorns and then solve those equations simultaneously. Using distance information and the coordinates of F_1 and F_2 yields these equations for the broadcast circles (see fig. 11):

$$F_1: \qquad x^2 + (y - 6)^2 = 4^2$$

$$\text{or}$$

$$x^2 + y^2 - 12y = -20$$

and

$$F_2: \qquad (x - 1)^2 + y^2 = 5^2$$

$$\text{or}$$

$$x^2 - 2x + y^2 = 24$$

The simultaneous solution of these two equations is the line $y = (1/6)x + (11/3)$. This expression for y can be substituted into either circular equation to determine the two x-coordinates where the circles intersect. Substituting into the expanded equation for F_2, we find that

$$x^2 - 2x + \left(\frac{1}{6}x + \frac{11}{3}\right)^2 = 24,$$

which simplifies to

$$37x^2 - 28x - 380 = 0,$$

whose solutions are $x = 3.605$ or $x = -2.849$. When these values are returned to the linear equation, the ordered pairs that represent the intersection points of the two circles are $(3.605, 4.268)$ and $(-2.849, 3.192)$.

How did the navigator know to choose the first of these ordered pairs as the ship's correct position on the basis of record 1? Perhaps the navigator knew that the ship was farther from Duluth than was indicated by the ordered pair $(-2.849, 3.192)$, or it might be that the navigator recognized that the ship was not as close to shore as was indicated by the rejected ordered pair.

We could have used other ways to determine the ship's position on the basis of the information in the first transmission record. Perhaps your students will suggest using a scale drawing and a compass to draw the two transmission circles. Depending on the desired degree of accuracy—is it essential to calculate the ship's position to within a thousandth of a unit?—a compass construction furnishes an adequate position fix.

Question 3 on student page 56 shows the navigator's work in beginning to fix the ship's position from transmission 4. Students can determine locations S_4 and S_5 using any acceptable method. Assuming that the ship does not travel in an erratic path, the foregoing analytic method yields $S_4 = (7.993, 5.666)$ and $S_5 = (9, 6)$.

Question 4 on student page 56 can be used to reinforce the two-dimensional time-of-arrival positioning methods explored thus far. Although signal reception times are provided from four foghorns, no more than three are necessary to ensure an accurate position fix. In fact, if we assume that the ship is indeed on the lake and not on shore, a correct position fix can be made by using information from only two foghorns. The correct location of the ship is at $(5, 8)$, which may be closer to the shore than the ship's captain has intended!

Clock Error in Two Dimensions

The sketch on student page 57 illustrates the impact of receiver-clock error on position fixing in a two-dimensional system. Problem 5 is presented to elicit one or more approaches to determining an accurate position fix in that setting. The discussion that follows illustrates one approach to solving the problem; students should be encouraged to generate others.

In figure 13, the Geometer's Sketchpad was used to create a scale drawing, with 1 cm = 1 mi. Using the signal transmission times given in the problem and

Technology Tip: *Software such as the Geometer's Sketchpad or Cabri Geometry II can be used to sketch the situation and make accurate estimates of point locations. Figures 12 and 13 were created using the Geometer's Sketchpad. The software also calculated coordinates of ordered pairs and generated equations for lines and circles, as shown here. With this tool, the navigator can model each of the transmission records by dragging points E and F on the circumferences of the circles to change the radii of the broadcast circles. All calculations are updated as the radii are changed.*

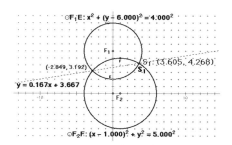

Fig. 12. Ordered pairs representing the intersection of the two circles

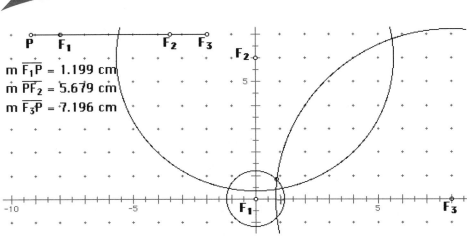

Fig. 13. Scale drawing created by the Geometer's Sketchpad. The common point appears to be within the region enclosed by the three circles near the point (1, 1). The receiver clock is running fast.

Technology Tip: *Dynamic geometry software allows students to represent the situation with a geometric model and to visualize the effect of clock error on the system.*

Teaching Tip: *Since the clock is running fast, the segments PF₁, PF₂, and PF₃ overestimate the distances from the respective transmitters. Decreasing the lengths of the segments allows us to estimate the true distances.*

186 000 miles per second as the speed of light—the speed at which radio waves also travel—we determined the radius of each broadcast transmission circle ($d_1 = 1.1904$ mi, $d_2 = 5.6637$ mi, $d_3 = 7.1908$ mi). The segment in the upper-left corner of figure 13 was constructed with points F_1, F_2, and F_3 on the segment, and the points were dragged until the segment lengths, whose measures are shown, corresponded as closely as possible to the calculated radii of the broadcast transmission circles.

The transmitter locations F_1, F_2, and F_3 were positioned on the grid, and circles were constructed with those points as centers and the segments PF_1, PF_2, and PF_3 as radii. Although accuracy was limited by the precision of measurements in the software, the construction shows that the three circles do not intersect in a common point, indicating the presence of receiver-clock error.

To approximate the location of the ship, point P in the upper-left corner was moved closer to each of the points F_1, F_2, and F_3 on the segment until it appeared that the three circles shared one common point, near (1, 1) on the grid. Sketchpad was then used to identify this common point, whose coordinates were given as (0.940, 0.560), the approximate location of the ship. The new values for the three radii, as given by the software, were $PF_1 = 1.094$ cm, $F_2 = 5.573$ cm, and $F_3 = 7.091$ cm. Again, accuracy was limited by the precision of the software.

A first estimate of the clock error can be made by subtracting the estimates of distance taken from the construction (where 1 cm = 1 mi) from the distances that were calculated from the reported transmission times. Each pair of values yields a difference of approximately 0.09 mile, the amount by which the distance from the transmitters was overestimated. Traveling at the speed of 186 000 mi/sec, the signals required approximately 0.0000004 second (four 10-millionths of a second) to traverse 0.09 mile. Even the most minute clock error has a profound effect when light or radio signals are involved.

Further Exploration

Mathematical Connection: *More advanced students can explore the effect of changing the amount of receiver-clock error. The interpretation involves analyzing the equation of a hyperbola.*

The Geometer's Sketchpad can be used to carry out an additional exploration of the scale drawing. Highlight the intersection points of each pair of circles and turn on the Sketchpad command "trace points." Point P on the segment in the upper-left corner of the screen can then be moved back and forth along the segment, allowing the intersection points to be traced. The locus of those points is shown in figure 14, with the three circles hidden from view to allow a clearer look at the locus of the traced points. It appears that each pair of transmitter points has a hyperbola associated with it. Can we account for that phenomenon?

Mission Mathematics: Grades 9–12

What is it about hyperbolas that may relate to the context we are exploring? (Recall the definition of a hyperbola: the set of all points in the plane that have a constant absolute difference in distance from two fixed points.)

To verify the conjecture that the locus of intersection points is a hyperbola, concentrate on the apparent hyperbola with foci at F_1 and F_3. Segments F_1A and F_3A have been added to figure 15. The lengths of these segments correspond to the radii of circles F_1 and F_3, respectively, and represent the distances from the signal transmitters to the ship when calculated with some unknown receiver-clock error. Letting r_1 and r_3 represent the true distance from each transmitter to the ship and letting e represent the error distance common to each distance calculation give

$$F_1A = r_1 + e$$

and

$$F_3A = r_3 + e.$$

Look at the absolute difference of these values:

$$|r_1 - r_3| = |r_1 + e - (r_3 + e)| = |F_1A - F_3A|$$

Regardless of the error distance introduced through receiver-clock error, a constant difference remains in the calculated distances from each pair of transmitters to the ship. The set of points that satisfies this condition generates a hyperbola, as we informally observed through the Sketchpad trace points.

As suggested by the trace points of the three hyperbolas, if we can determine the intersection point of the hyperbolas we will have determined the possible location of the ship. With accurate scale drawings, we can determine a precise position fix. To determine the hyperbolas' intersection points analytically, we first need equations for the hyperbolas. We again use the hyperbola associated with F_1 and F_3, this time to generate its equation.

Recall that in the hyperbola with center at $P = (h, k)$ and equation

$$\frac{(x-h)^2}{a^2} - \frac{(y-k)^2}{b^2} = 1,$$

each focus is c units from (h, k), each vertex is a units from (h, k), and $a^2 + b^2 = c^2$ (fig. 16). For the situation on the navigator's map (fig. 17), we have foci at $(0, 0)$ and $(8, 0)$. The center is at $(4, 0)$, and $c = 4$ represents half the distance from F_1 to F_3. We determine a by calculating half the constant difference $|F_1A - F_3A|$, using the signal-transmission times given in the problem:

$$F_1A = 0.00000640 \text{ sec} \cdot 186\,000 \text{ mi/sec} = 1.19040000 \text{ mi}$$

and

$$F_3A = 0.00003866 \text{ sec} \cdot 186\,000 \text{ mi/sec} = 7.19076000 \text{ mi}.$$

This result shows that $|F_1A - F_3A|$ is very close to 6 miles, resulting in the value $a = 3$ mi. Since $b^2 = c^2 - a^2$, where $c = 4$ and $a = 3$, we determine that $b = \sqrt{7}$ and that the equation of our hyperbola is

$$\frac{(x-4)^2}{9} - \frac{(y-0)^2}{7} = 1.$$

In a similar manner, we can show that the hyperbola involving transmitter points F_1 and F_2 has the equation

$$\frac{(y-3)^2}{5} - \frac{(x-0)^2}{4} = 1.$$

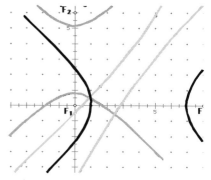

Fig. 14. Locus of intersection points

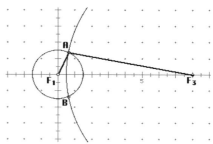

Fig. 15. Signal transmission circles

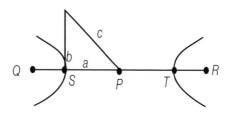

Fig. 16. Basic hyperbola relationships

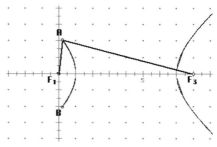

Fig. 17. Navigator's map

Plotting these two hyperbolas with a graphing utility reveals an intersection point with coordinates (0.9406, 0.5290). Note that this ordered pair is close to the one approximated using Sketchpad's scale drawing.

Finally, we can determine the receiver-clock error by comparing the transmitter broadcast radius with the true distance from a transmitter to the ship. Focusing on F_1, we already have computed 1.19040000 miles as the transmitter broadcast radius that includes clock error. Using the foregoing ordered pairs, we can calculate the true distance from F_1 to the ship to be 1.07916298 miles. The difference is 0.11123702 mile. Dividing this result by 186 000 mi/sec yields a clock error of 0.0000006 second. The receiver clock runs 0.0000006 second fast, which agrees quite well with the error estimated from the Sketchpad activity.

Solutions:

Student page 58 shows three sets of receiver-reception times. Students should use methods of their choice to determine in each case the receiver position and the amount of receiver-clock error, if any. Using the approach described earlier, we have these solutions:

6. Receiver position: (–2/3, 11.9257); receiver-clock error: 0.0000025 second fast

7. Receiver position: (2.17458, 1.95609); receiver-clock error: 0.000005 second slow

8. Receiver position: (0, 3); receiver-clock error: 0.000008 second fast.

Looking Back

Use question 9 on student page 58 both to summarize and to generalize the work completed in two-dimensional time-of-arrival positioning.

If no clock error is present, signal broadcast-transmission times can be used to determine broadcast-transmission circles. With no error, the three circles will have one common point. The common point can be determined analytically by determining the intersection points and the lines from the equations of the broadcast-transmission circles. Scale drawings, from pencil-and-paper or computer-generated models, can also be used to generate position estimates.

If receiver-clock error does occur, scale-drawing estimates can be used that employ a dynamic constant change in the radii of the broadcast-transmission circles. As shown in the Sketchpad figures associated with the earlier discussion, this technique provides reasonable position estimates. Analytic techniques that require determining intersection points of hyperbolas can also be employed, especially when coordinate systems are established that place two or more transmitters on the same horizontal or vertical line.

DETERMINING POSITION IN THREE DIMENSIONS

This set of activities completes students' conceptualization of the mathematics of time-of-arrival positioning by extending and applying the triangulation concepts and procedures developed in one and two dimensions. The setting is a three-dimensional system situated on Earth. A hiker uses time-of-arrival positioning to determine her position while hiking in the mountains. Radio waves traveling at 186 000 miles per second are broadcast from a constellation of satellites orbiting Earth. The signals are transmitted to the hiker's hand-held receiver, where they are used to determine location on the Earth's surface (fig. 18). In essence, students are presented the components of NAVSTAR's GPS.

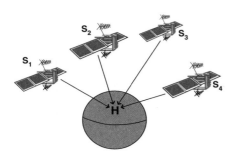

Fig. 18. Satellites in orbit transmit signals to a hand-held receiver.

Use student page 58 to begin a class discussion of a three-dimensional time-of-arrival positioning system. Students who have successfully completed activities in one- and two-dimensional positioning should be prepared to identify the fundamental components of a three-dimensional system:

- Broadcast signals from known locations

- Signal receptions at the unknown location

- Determination of elapsed time for signal broadcasts

- Calculation of distances between known and unknown locations

- Position fixes based on calculated distances

- Allowance for clock error within a system

These components form the basis for the discussion of a three-dimensional time-of-arrival positioning system. The discussion of the triangulation process applied to a three-dimensional system should focus on concepts rather than on calculations. After students have reviewed their work in one and two dimensions, use questions such as the following to help students extend their understanding:

- How can we calculate the distance between two points in a three-dimensional coordinate system? [We extend distance calculations from two dimensions to three by repeated application of the Pythagorean theorem (see fig. 19).]

- What geometric shape represents the set of all possible locations that are a known distance from a satellite? [A sphere of radius r]

- Signals from how many different satellites will be required to pinpoint one unique point of signal reception? [Two spheres can have zero, one, or an infinite number of points in common. In the last case, the set of points represents a circle. But with three spheres, if the time-of-arrival positioning system has no errors, the three spheres have exactly one point in common, the desired position fix.]

- If we want to correct for clock error, signals from how many satellites will be required? [A fourth satellite is required to fix a unique position.]

To help students represent more formally the mathematics of a three-dimensional time-of-arrival positioning system, student page 59 asks for a system of equations that could be solved to determine location in a three-dimensional coordinate system (fig. 20). Such a system follows:

$$\begin{cases} D_1 = \sqrt{\left(x - x_1\right)^2 + \left(y - y_1\right)^2 + \left(z - z_1\right)^2} \\ D_2 = \sqrt{\left(x - x_2\right)^2 + \left(y - y_2\right)^2 + \left(z - z_2\right)^2} \\ D_3 = \sqrt{\left(x - x_3\right)^2 + \left(y - y_3\right)^2 + \left(z - z_3\right)^2} \end{cases}$$

Some students may be motivated to solve this set of equations for the unknown point (x, y, z), whereas others may explore ways to use technology to approximate the values for x, y, and z. The emphasis, however, should be on using the three-dimensional coordinate system as one way to represent students' ideas mathematically. The problems on student page 60 illustrate the calculations of time and distance that are part of a three-dimensional time-of-arrival positioning system; they may lead to a class discussion of the impact of clock error in a GPS, where even a fraction-of-a-second difference translates into hundreds of miles (or more) of error.

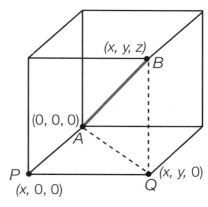

Fig. 19

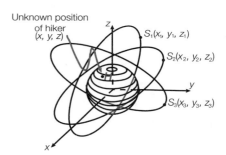

Fig. 20. Three-dimensional positioning system

The tasks in which students engage must encourage them to reason about mathematical ideas, to make connections, and to formulate, grapple with, and solve problems.

(NCTM 1990, p. 32)

Solutions:

1. (a) 18 456 mi ÷ 186 000 mi/sec = 0.099226 sec. (b) The receiver clock will determine a travel time of 0.099326 second. Then 0.099326 sec • 186 000 mi/sec = 18 474.6 mi. The error is slightly less than 19 miles. (c) A difference of 378 miles exists between the actual and computed

distance, and 378 mi ÷ 186 000 mi/sec = 0.002032 sec. The receiver clock is 0.002032 second slow.

2. $$D = \sqrt{(2\,024 - 1\,025)^2 + (1\,520 - 0)^2 + (13\,164 - 3\,825)^2} = 9\,514.5 \text{ mi.}$$

It will take 0.051153 second for the signal to travel that distance.

GPS APPLICATIONS

Use question 3 on student page 60 to preview the GPS-application activities, which involve a transition from the Cartesian coordinate system that we have been using to a system based on latitude and longitude. The reality of GPS is that a different coordinate system builds the framework for the location and navigation information available on GPS readouts. There are actually several coordinate systems from which location can be reported through a GPS receiver, but the system most familiar to many GPS users is the system of longitude and latitude expressed in degrees, minutes, and seconds. Together with a measure of altitude, typically expressed in feet above or below sea level, GPS receivers report location and navigation information that is familiar to its users. These three measures form the basis for many maps and other location and navigation aids in use today.

The activities that conclude this unit are intended to help you and your students become familiar with applications of the information available from a GPS receiver. Although the applications focus on aspects of location and navigation, GPS can be used in many more ways in personal, recreational, commercial, agricultural, and governmental settings.

Lake Superior

Application 1 brings students back to the Lake Superior setting, this time with a more detailed map and instructions to plot a ship's course on Lake Superior on the basis of six GPS readouts. The image in figure 21 shows approximate locations of the ship determined by the GPS readout. Students are asked to determine the direction of the ship in part so they will focus on the date information shown on the GPS readouts. Because the two readouts dated 24 April 1997 are the two closest to Duluth, it is a safe assumption that the ship is moving toward the harbor. A specific path, however, such as the one shown on the map, is only a suggestion. We have no information indicating the ship's location other than the six GPS readouts. In particular, we do not know the elapsed time between GPS readings. In subsequent applications, students will encounter and interpret time as well as date information in the GPS readouts.

The prime meridian through Greenwich, England, supplies a reference circle for east and west longitude measurement; the equator is a reference circle for north and south latitude measurement.

The curriculum should be infused with examples of how geometry is used in recreations..., in practical tasks..., in the sciences..., and in the arts....

(NCTM 1989, p. 157)

Teaching Tip: Note that the longitude and latitude on the maps are expressed in degrees to the nearest tenth of a degree, whereas the sample readouts from the GPS units express longitude and latitude in degrees and minutes or in degrees, minutes, and seconds. You will need to bring this distinction to the attention of your students and help them make conversions when necessary.

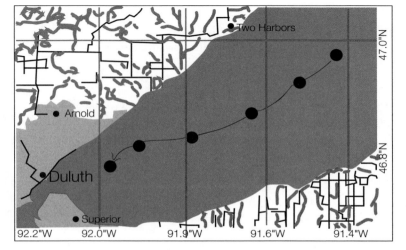

Fig. 21. Map showing locations of the ship

Snake River

This activity complements the previous one. Here, we are shown locations on the map along the Snake River from which students must make longitude and latitude estimates. The following are estimates of the latitude and longitude for each point, generated using mapping software:

① 43°25′ N, 110°51′ W   ④ 43°23′ N, 110°46′ W

② 43°24′ N, 110°50′ W   ⑤ 43°23′ N, 110°45′ W

③ 43°24′ N, 110°49′ W   ⑥ 43°22′ N, 110°44′ W

Teaching Tip: *For greater precision in solving these problems, secure a larger map of the region from an atlas or a road map. Maps also can be downloaded from the Internet or from CD-ROM software.*

Admittedly, only very small differences can be found among these values, which should raise questions that you may want to discuss with your students.

• With the information shown on the map, how can we make our estimates? Why has a second map been included?

• What level of accuracy is acceptable for our estimates? In a later application, you will encounter GPS readings expressed in degrees, minutes, and decimal parts of a second. Of what level of accuracy can we be assured in a GPS read-out? How does the level of accuracy in a GPS measure of longitude and latitude relate to the determination of distances on the basis of those readings?

San Antonio–Phoenix

In this application the GPS readouts include more information. In addition to the date, the first line of the position readout shows the time in hours, minutes, and seconds; the letter Z indicates that the unit has been set up for use in the air (rather than on land (U) or sea (G)). The displayed time is Greenwich mean time (GMT); when the receiver is set to show local time, no symbol—Z, U, or G—is displayed. Line 4 shows the altitude of the GPS unit. The symbol MSL represents height above mean sea level, here expressed in feet.

The map (fig. 22) shows a flight path based on estimates of position using the GPS data. Because readings ❶ and ❷ show identical values except for a time difference of 25 minutes, it seems likely that the aircraft did not move from the San Antonio airport during that time. If we assume that this is true and that reading ❽ occurred on touchdown at the Phoenix airport, the flight lasted 1 hour, 32 minutes, 35 seconds. On the basis of the altitudes shown in the readouts, we can conclude that the plane must have reached an altitude of at least 29 976 feet. It may have flown higher.

Teaching Tip: *With the increasing popularity of GPS among drivers, boaters, hunters, and others, it is possible that students in your class will have had first-hand experience with GPS and may even own GPS units that they can demonstrate.*

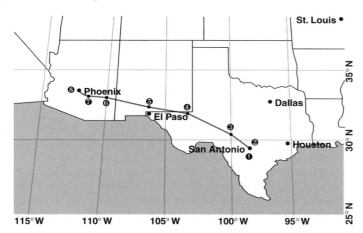

Fig. 22. Map showing flight plan from San Antonio to Phoenix

Anaheim

The fourth application extends the task of estimating location using longitude and latitude to an analysis of a situation for which GPS data may provide helpful information. The package-delivery setting is used to highlight the increasingly popular use of GPS and other location and navigation tools in transportation settings. The setting described here is a much simplified version of what may be done in the real world, yet it offers a rich setting for analysis and communication.

Note that the longitude and latitude of location D are given, although this information is not necessary for completing the problem; it is provided as a reference point if the need arises. With no longitude or latitude lines shown on the map, students will need to compare the longitudes and latitudes for the GPS readouts. Since the six points of delivery are shown on the map, students can match the GPS readouts with the map locations by independently ordering the set of six longitudes and the set of six latitudes. Location ❻, for instance, has the northernmost latitude and the easternmost longitude. Similar relative positioning analyses result in the matches shown in figure 23.

28APR97 08:45:12	28APR97 08:52:21	28APR97 09:03:15
LAT N 33° 51.48' ❻	LAT N 33° 51.30' ❺	LAT N 33° 51.06' ❸
LON W 117° 51.54'	LON W 117° 51.90'	LON W 117° 52.86'
28APR97 09:11:52	28APR97 09:17:20	28APR97 09:31:01
LAT N 33° 50.52' ❷	LAT N 33° 50.70' ❶	LAT N 33° 50.58' ❹
LON W 117° 53.28'	LON W 117° 53.76'	LON W 117° 52.08'

Fig. 23. GPS readouts

Teaching Tip: *Students can investigate and report on local businesses that employ GPS in their operations.*

With this information we can trace a path that connects the locations in the order determined. Starting at the distribution center (D), the driver traveled to locations 6, 5, 3, 2, 1, and 4, in that order, and finished the deliveries by returning to D. The map in figure 24 shows one of many paths that reasonably represent this sequence of deliveries.

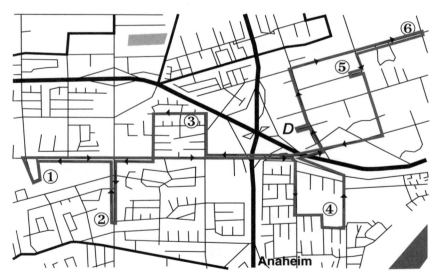

Fig. 24. Map of package-delivery route

Just as the driver could have followed several possible paths in completing the six deliveries, we could find ourselves with several questions and concerns that were raised by our evaluation of the route:

- The total distance traveled may vary from one route to another.

- The map does not clearly show underpass or overpass options near what apparently are two freeways transversing Anaheim, nor does the map indicate areas of known or potential traffic congestion.

Assessment Tip: *Students should give a rationale to support their choices of possible delivery routes.*

- We also do not know whether the map shows a primarily commercial or residential area.

- After carefully looking at distances traveled, students may also question the elapsed times between deliveries. Again, many unknowns may account for the travel time being longer than we may anticipate.

The alternative routes that students suggest should be accompanied by a justification and a rationale that address one or more of the types of concerns discussed here. Interested students can pursue some of these questions in more detail. They can search reference materials for information about this part of Anaheim or talk to a local delivery service about the factors that have an impact on times and routes for deliveries.

LOOKING BACK AND LOOKING AHEAD

Following the activities, students should reflect on some aspect of the GPS that they have studied. Those interested in investigating GPS further can select some of the following activities:

1. Review the concepts and procedures for using time-of-arrival positioning systems. Identify the essential components of any such system and show how mathematics is used to make accurate position fixes.

2. Use dynamic geometry such as the Geometer's Sketchpad or Cabri Geometry II to create an interactive application that you can use to make position fixes in one, two, or three dimensions.

3. Write a program for a graphing calculator that you can use to make position fixes in one, two, or three dimensions.

4. Read one of the following articles on GPS and present a written or oral summary to your class:

   - Brogdon, Bill. "Space-Age Trail Blazers." *Outdoor Life,* August 1993, pp. 53–55.

   - Chien, Philip. "You are Here." *Popular Mechanics,* November 1993, pp. 50–52.

   - Herring, Thomas A. "The Global Positioning System." *Scientific American,* February 1996, pp. 44–50.

   - Vest, Floyd, William Diedrich, and Kenneth Vos. "Mathematics and the Global Positioning System." *Consortium,* Spring 1994, HiMap pull-out section.

   - Wright, Ed. "GPS Takes a Vacation." *GPS World,* June 1995, pp. 22–30.

5. Look through recent issues of *GPS World* (ISSN 1048-5104) and pick out a GPS application that is of interest to you. Use that application as a basis for a research report to your class. Try to include an interview with someone who actually uses GPS in his or her professional or recreational activities.

6. Create a three-dimensional, scale-model representation of the spheres of intersection that result when three or four satellite signals are used to fix a position on or near Earth. Identify the geometric shapes that result when two or more spheres intersect.

In completing the activities involving the mathematics and applications of GPS, students have—

- *used one-, two-, and three-dimensional coordinate systems to identify positions;*
- *used time of arrival for sound waves and radio waves to fix unknown positions using triangulation;*
- *used GPS-receiver readouts to solve location and navigation problems.*

MATHEMATICS AND APPLICATIONS OF A GLOBAL POSITIONING SYSTEM

Components of a Global Positioning System (GPS)

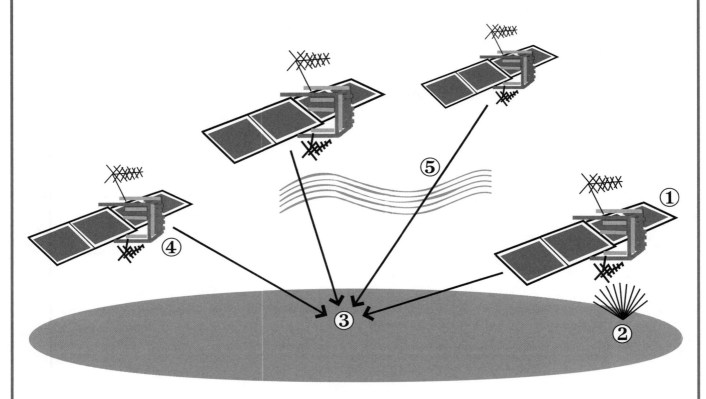

At the heart of a GPS is *triangulation,* the determination of an unknown position using distances from known positions. A GPS receiver uses signal-transmission times from orbiting satellites to calculate distances from those satellites, which in turn are used to determine receiver position.

① In the U.S. system called NAVSTAR (**Nav**igation **S**atellite **T**iming **a**nd **R**anging), twenty-four satellites orbit Earth, giving GPS users at least five satellites visible from any point on Earth.

② A worldwide monitoring system tracks the GPS satellites and generates an

orbital model for each satellite. A master control station in Colorado sends to each satellite orbital data and clock corrections that are relayed to GPS users.

③ GPS users on or near Earth use GPS receivers to convert satellite signals to position, velocity, and time estimates.

④ Each satellite has four atomic clocks, accurate to within a billionth of a second a year.

⑤ The speed of GPS satellite signals may be altered as they travel through the atmosphere. At the speed of light, even slight changes in transmission speed introduce significant errors into the system.

DETERMINING POSITION IN ONE DIMENSION

The diagram below shows a bird's-eye view of a football-field sideline. A coach is at point C on the sideline. He is wearing a headset with a special receiver. The receiver picks up sound waves that are broadcast at one-minute intervals from a transmitter located at point T at one end of the sideline. If the coach moves only along the sideline, how can a transmitter-receiver system like this one be used to determine his position?

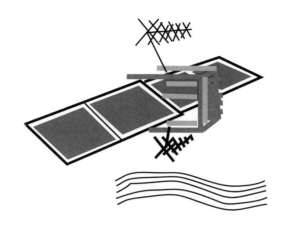

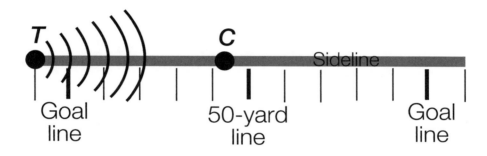

Answer the following questions assuming that sound travels at 1100 feet a second:

1. If the coach is at the 50-yard line, how long will it take a sound wave to travel from T to C?

2. A sound wave requires 0.14 second to travel from T to C. What is the coach's position?

3. The coach is at the 30-yard line. What *two* travel times are possible for a sound wave to move from the transmitter to the coach?

4. Determine the time difference in a sound wave traveling from T to *each* goal line.

5. Sound waves are broadcast from T at one-minute intervals starting on the hour. The coach's receiver includes a clock synchronized with the one in the transmitter. Determine the missing information in the table below.

Time Sent (transmitter) (hr:min:sec)	Time Received (receiver) (hr:min:sec)	Coach's Postion
0:02:00.0000	0:02:00.0762	(a)
0:25:00.0000	0:25:00.1238	(b)
0:57:00.0000	(c)	12-yard line farther from T

What happens if a receiver clock is not precisely synchronized with a transmitter clock? Given an asynchronous relationship between the two clocks, how can we modify the time-of-arrival system to ensure that precise locations are determined?

For example, suppose that the clock in the coach's receiver is, unknowingly, running 0.01 second fast. If a signal is broadcast from the transmitter at 1:00:00.0000 and the receiver registers its reception at 1:00:00.1247, the signal actually took 0.1147 second to go from the transmitter to the receiver.

Using only the receiver clock, without knowing that it is running 0.01 second fast, we would have erroneously determined that the coach was at C_e, near the 36-yard line: 0.1247 sec × 1100 ft/sec ÷ 3 ft/yd = 45.7233 yd from T_1. The signal, however, traveled only 0.1147 second, positioning the coach at C_a, near the 32-yard line: 0.1147 sec × 1100 ft/sec ÷ 3 ft/yd = 42.0567 yd from T_1.

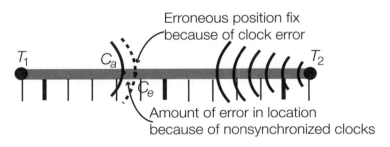

Erroneous position fix because of clock error

Amount of error in location because of nonsynchronized clocks

6. How can a signal from T_2 be used with the existing system to fix the coach's position in the foregoing example?

7. The coach is positioned at the 40-yard line that is closer to the transmitter at T_1. Because the coach's receiver is not synchronized with the transmitters, using only the T_1 transmission will erroneously locate the coach at the 50-yard line.

   (a) Determine how fast or how slow the receiver clock is running.

   (b) A broadcast is sent from T_2 at 1:27:00.0000. What will the receiver clock read when it receives this transmission?

8. Sound waves are broadcast from T_1 and T_2 at 0:23:00.0000. The coach's receiver records the T_1 transmission at 0:23:00.0892 and the T_2 transmission at 0:23:00.2981. Determine the coach's position and justify that the coach's receiver is not synchronized with the clocks in the transmitters. Determine how fast or slow the receiver clock is running.

9. Generalize a method for using a one-dimensional time-of-arrival positioning system to determine accurately the location of point P on a number line and the amount of receiver-clock error when transmitters are located at known coordinates X_1 and X_2 on the number line.

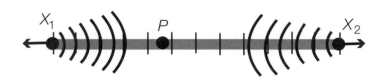

DETERMINING POSITION IN TWO DIMENSIONS

A sailing vessel travels on Lake Superior from the harbor at Duluth. The diagram shows the lake, the ship, and the location of four foghorns. The ship, *S,* moves out onto the lake from Duluth. On board is a receiver that records sound waves from foghorns. The receiver picks up sound waves that are broadcast on the minute at one-minute intervals from foghorn transmitters located at fixed points F_1, F_2, F_3, and F_4.

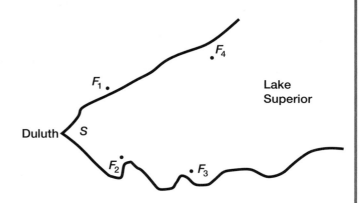

1. How can such a transmitter-receiver system be used to determine the ship's position?

Here is a simplified version of a map that the ship's navigator might use to record and track the ship's position. Note the use of rectangular coordinates with grid marks each 1 mile apart.

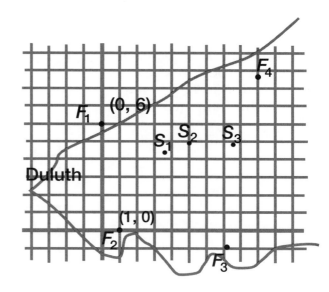

2. Study the table below. It shows data recorded after the ship left the harbor. The ship sailed at 15:12:30.0000. What calculations and assumptions has the navigator made to fix the ship's position?

Record No.	Signal Reception Times		Foghorn District (mi)		Ship's Position	
	F_1	F_2	F_1	F_2	X	Y
1	15:40:19.2000	15:40:24.0000	4.00	5.00	3.605	4.268
2	15:50:24.0000	15:50:28.8000	5.00	6.00	4.810	4.635
3	16:10:36.0000	16:10:38.4000	7.50	8.00	7.403	4.796
4	16:20:38.4000	16:20:43.2000				
5	16:30:43.2000	16:30:48.0000				

3. The three lightly shaded dots on the map at the right indicate the first three position fixes made by the navigator, using the data from the foregoing navigator's table. The navigator has begun to fix a fourth positon. Complete the data entry for records 4 and 5 in the navigator's table. Locate the fourth and fifth position points on the map.

What assumptions have you made in determining the positions associated with table entries 4 and 5?

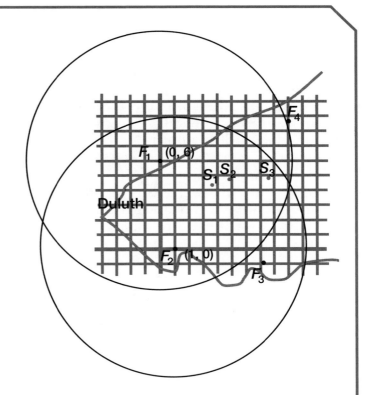

4. A ship has lost its bearing on Lake Superior. The only information to aid navigation is the transmission data, shown below, from the four foghorns. Each foghorn broadcasts a signal every minute on the minute. Determine the ship's location and show the point on the grid at the right. Is the ship in trouble?

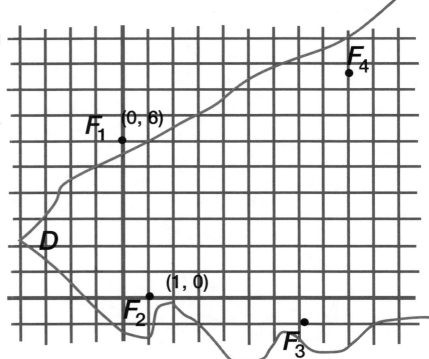

Signal Reception Times

F_1 23:09:25.8488

F_2 23:09:42.9325

F_3 23:09:44.2538

F_4 23:09:19.7909

What if a receiver clock is not precisely synchronized with a transmitter clock? Given an asynchronous relationship between the two clocks, how can we modify a two-dimensional time-of-arrival system to ensure precise location determination?

A one-second error in a receiver clock translates into an error of 1100 feet in position fixing when sound waves are broadcast. When radio signals are used, a one-second error represents 186 000 miles! Here is a sketch to represent an attempted position fix with a receiver clock that is running slightly fast.

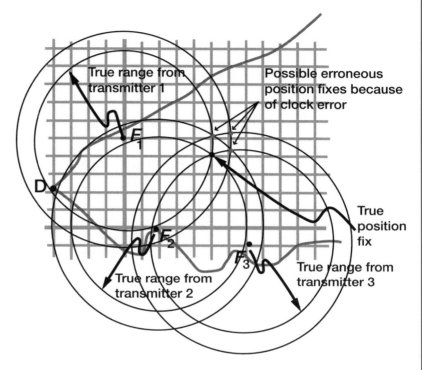

♦ How will a ship's navigator know whether there is receiver-clock error?

♦ How will a ship's navigator know whether the receiver clock is running fast or slow?

♦ What must the navigator do to account for the receiver-clock error to make an accurate position fix?

♦ How can the amount of receiver-clock error be determined?

5. Here is a navigator's map and data table from a voyage on another lake. Use the information to determine the ship's position and the amount of receiver-clock error. Grid lines on the map are 1 mile apart, and each transmitter broadcasts radio signals traveling at 186 000 miles per second.

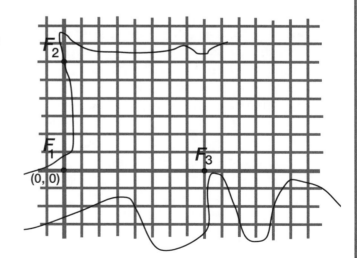

Signal Transmission Times (sec)

F_1	0.00000640
F_2	0.00003045
F_3	0.00003866

For problems 6–8, you are shown transmitter locations and signal reception times. Use the information to determine the receiver's position and the amount of receiver-clock error in each case. Assume that each transmitter broadcasts a radio signal every minute on the minute, that radio signals travel at 186 000 miles per second, and that the broadcast-transmitter clocks in each set are synchronized.

6.

	Transmitter Location	Signal Reception Time
T_1	(–8, 0)	8:36:00.000 077 77
T_2	(–2, 0)	8:36:00.000 067 02
T_3	(10, 0)	8:36:00.000 088 52

7.

	Transmitter Location	Signal Reception Time
T_1	(–5, 0)	1:41:00.000 034 98
T_2	(5, 0)	1:41:00.000 013 48
T_3	(0, –3)	1:41:00.000 024 10
T_4	(0, 3)	1:41:00.000 007 97

8.

	Transmitter Location	Signal Reception Time
T_1	(–8, 0)	16:21:00.000 053 94
T_2	(2, 0)	16:21:00.000 027 38
T_3	(0, 6)	16:21:00.000 024 13

9. Describe how to use a two-dimensional time-of-arrival positioning system to determine the location of point P on a coordinate plane when broadcast transmitters are located at known coordinates F_1, F_2, and F_3 on the plane. Consider the case with clock error as well as the case without clock error.

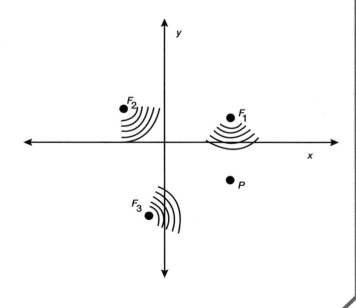

DETERMINING POSITION IN THREE DIMENSIONS

A mountain climber is hiking in the Rocky Mountains. The figure shows Earth, the hiker at point H, and radio signals transmitted from four satellites, S_1, S_2, S_3, and S_4. Each satellite orbits approximately 11 000 miles above Earth, and the hiker has a hand-held unit that receives the satellites' signals. A coded signal from each satellite includes the time its signal was transmitted as well as information about its position. The hiker's receiver records the time of arrival of each radio signal. How can such a transmitter-receiver system be used to determine the hiker's position?

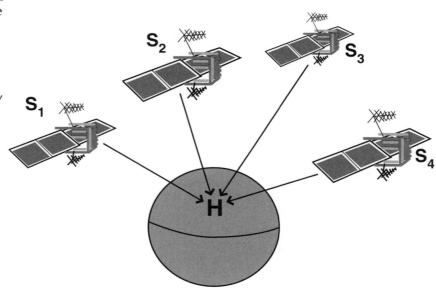

Use the three-dimensional coordinate system shown here to write a system of equations that can be solved to determine the position of the hiker at point H (x, y, z) in the mock-up below. The center of Earth is at the coordinate (0, 0, 0).

Equations
_____

Unknown position of hiker (x, y, z)

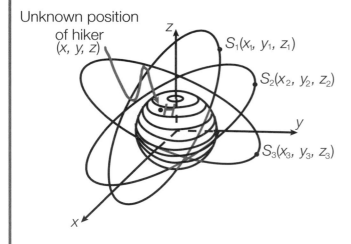

$S_1(x_1, y_1, z_1)$

$S_2(x_2, y_2, z_2)$

$S_3(x_3, y_3, z_3)$

Radio signals from an Earth-orbiting satellite travel at 186 000 miles per second. The (x, y, z) coordinates used at the right are expressed in miles and refer to an Earth-centered three-dimensional system. The atomic clocks in the NAVSTAR GPS satellites are accurate to within a billionth of a second a year, whereas the clocks in GPS receivers are typically much less accurate.

1. A hand-held GPS receiver is 18 456 miles from a specific satellite.

   (a) How long will it take for a signal to travel from the satellite to the receiver?

   (b) If the clock in the hand-held unit runs 0.0001 second fast, what is the error in the distance calculated from the satellite to the receiver?

   (c) The GPS receiver calculated the receiver-to-satellite distance to be 18 078 miles. If receiver-clock error is the only factor affecting accuracy, what is the receiver-clock error?

2. A hiker, H, is positioned on Earth at the point (1 025, 0, 3 825), and a satellite, S, is orbiting Earth at the point (2 024, 1 520, 13 164).

   (a) Use a coordinate system like the one shown on page 59 to estimate the location of points H and S.

   (b) How far is S from H?

   (c) How long will it take a satellite signal to travel from S to H?

3. A location readout from a GPS receiver, like the one shown here, is typically expressed in longitude, latitude, and altitude. On the screen of the receiver used in this example, the letter U on the first line indicates that the unit has been set up for use on land (rather than air (Z) or sea (G)) and that the displayed time is not offset from time at the

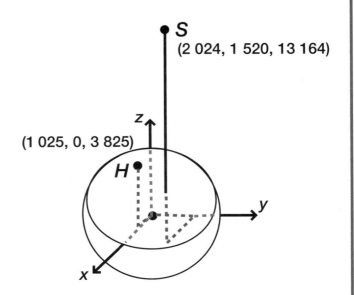

S
(2 024, 1 520, 13 164)

(1 025, 0, 3 825)

prime meridian through Greenwich, England (Greenwich mean time). When the receiver has been set up to show local time, no symbol—Z, U, or G—is displayed. Suggest reasons for the use of longitude, latitude, and altitude rather than (x, y, z) coordinates in GPS location readouts.

```
9   FEB97   12:15:07U
LAT   44°08′02.4″N
LON    74°31′15.6″W
MSL +1513FT
```

GPS APPLICATIONS

✦ Lake Superior

Here is a map of a portion of Lake Superior, together with six screens from a hand-held GPS unit that show longitude and latitude for a ship near the harbor. Use the GPS readings to mark the path and direction of the ship on the map.

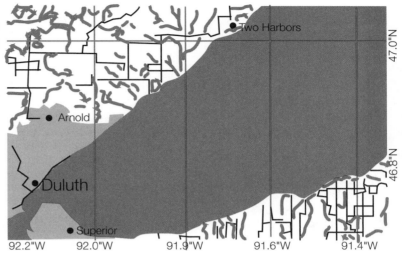

LAT N 46° 55.482'	LAT N 46° 52.094'	LAT N 46° 49.714'
LON W 91° 31.572'	LON W 91° 39.657'	LON W 91° 53.920'
date 23 APR 97	date 23 APR 97	date 24 APR 97
LAT N 46 ° 50.681'	LAT N 46° 58.613'	LAT N 46° 43.810'
LON W 91° 46.510'	LON W 91° 26.217'	LON W 91° 58.873'
date 23 APR 97	date 23 APR 97	date 24 APR 97

✦ Snake River

Here are two maps of a region near Jackson, Wyoming. A rafter carries a GPS unit with her on a float trip down the Snake River. She has taken readings at the six points marked on the second map.

Estimate the GPS longitude-and-latitude reading at each of the six points. Express each estimate using degrees and minutes.

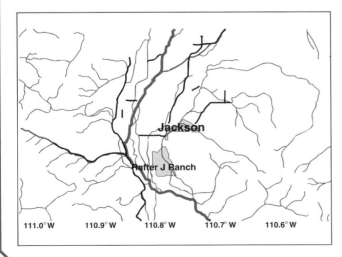

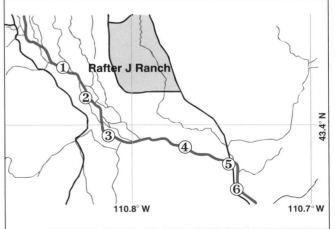

✦ San Antonio–Phoenix

Here is a map and readings from a hand-held GPS unit on board an aircraft flying from San Antonio to Phoenix. Use the GPS readings to chart on the map the flight path. Determine the length of the flight in hours, minutes, and seconds. What do you suppose occurred during the time that readings ❶ and ❷ were taken? What is the lowest possible maximum altitude the aircraft could have reached?

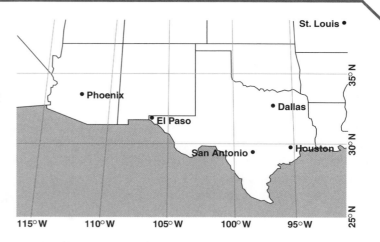

St. Louis •

• Phoenix

Dallas •

El Paso

San Antonio •   • Houston

35°N   30°N   25°N

115°W   110°W   105°W   100°W   95°W

08MAR97 02:12:10 Z LAT N 29° 23.043' LON W 98° 29.047' MSL +701 ft ❶	08MAR97 02:37:29 Z LAT N 29° 23.043' LON W 98° 29.047' MSL +701 ft ❷	08MAR97 02:55:23 Z LAT N 30° 13.679' LON W 100° 09.962' MSL +12842 ft ❸	08MAR97 03:17:01 Z LAT N 31° 43.620' LON W 103° 35.104' MSL +28976 ft ❹
08MAR97 03:28:42 Z LAT N 32° 20.221' LON W 106° 21.602' MSL +25212 ft ❺	08MAR97 03:52:38 Z LAT N 32° 54.011' LON W 109° 56.038' MSL +14922 ft ❻	08MAR97 04:02:11 Z LAT N 32° 54.361' LON W 111° 19.800' MSL +5480 ft ❼	08MAR97 04:10:04 Z LAT N 33° 32.585' LON W 112° 05.259' MSL +1090 ft ❽

✦ Anaheim

Here is a map of Anaheim, California, and GPS readings taken at the points marked ❶ through ❻ on the map. A local distribution center for American Package Systems (APS) is at point D (33.851°N, 117.871°W). Points ❶ through ❻ represent the locations of six deliveries made by an APS driver on a weekday morning. First, match the GPS readings with the delivery locations. Then, on the map, trace a possible route that the APS truck may have followed in making the six deliveries, beginning and ending the route at D.

After you have completed the route, evaluate it: Do you think that the driver took an efficient route? What additional information would you like to have to better carry out an evaluation? Provide one or more alternative routes that the driver could have followed that may have been more efficient.

28APR97 08:45:12 LAT N 33 ° 51.48' LON W 117° 51.54'	28APR97 08:52:21 LAT N 33 ° 51.30' LON W 117° 51.90'	28APR97 09:03:15 LAT N 33 ° 51.06' LON W 117° 52.86'
28APR97 09:11:52 LAT N 33 ° 50.52' LON W 117° 53.28'	28APR97 09:17:20 LAT N 33 ° 50.70' LON W 117° 53.76'	28APR97 09:31:01 LAT N 33 ° 50.58' LON W 117° 52.08'

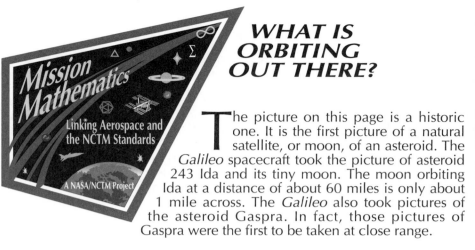

WHAT IS ORBITING OUT THERE?

The picture on this page is a historic one. It is the first picture of a natural satellite, or moon, of an asteroid. The *Galileo* spacecraft took the picture of asteroid 243 Ida and its tiny moon. The moon orbiting Ida at a distance of about 60 miles is only about 1 mile across. The *Galileo* also took pictures of the asteroid Gaspra. In fact, those pictures of Gaspra were the first to be taken at close range.

Most of humanity has had a limited knowledge of orbiting bodies in the solar system. The fact that Earth orbits the Sun is common knowledge. Likewise, it is widely understood that the other planets of the solar system orbit the Sun, too. However, the orbits of asteroids and comets, as well as of the satellites of the planets and other bodies, are less well known. NASA's solar system exploration is providing more data about the many celestial bodies that orbit larger celestial bodies or the Sun; thus, this information is becoming available to the general population.

At least fifty-four satellites orbit planets. The inner planets—Mercury, Venus, Earth, and Mars—have only three satellites. The Moon orbits Earth, and two irregularly shaped bodies orbit Mars. The Martian satellites are probably asteroids that were captured by the gravitational field of the planet. The outer planets—Jupiter, Saturn, Uranus, Neptune, and Pluto—have numerous satellites. Jupiter has at least sixteen, Saturn has seventeen, Uranus has fourteen, Neptune has two, and Pluto has one.

In addition to the planets, other celestial bodies orbit the Sun. Asteroids like the one pictured generally orbit the Sun in an area called the asteroid belt, which is between the orbits of Mars and Jupiter. More than 5000 asteroids have been named and cataloged. Although the belt of asteroids is generally between Mars and Jupiter, the orbits are not always aligned with the orbital planes of these planets. Thus, the orbits of the asteroids intersect the orbits of the planets. As a result, asteroids may pass very close to a planet and even be "caught" by the gravitational field of the planet and crash onto its surface. Some asteroids have Earth-orbit intersections. In 1989, asteroid 4581 Asclepius passed within 500 000 miles of Earth, a relatively small distance in solar system terms.

Comets, too, orbit the Sun. Less is known about comets because their very large orbits cause them to appear rarely. Comet orbits pass close to the Sun and extend deep into the solar system. Some comets have their point of greatest distance from the Sun in the region of the outer planets; for example, seventy-five comets have their farthest distance from the Sun somewhere near Jupiter. Since comet orbits have different farthest distances, the periods between the ability to observe the comets from Earth vary from 3.3 years, for Encke's comet, to thousands of years.

Since comets have predictable orbits, space scientists have been able to collect data about them from space probes. In 1985, the *Interplanetary Sun-Earth Explorer (ISEE) 3* was maneuvered into an encounter with comet P/Giacobini-Zinner. Perhaps the most famous comet because it appears every 76 years, Halley's comet was the target of flybys by spacecraft from three other space agencies during its last pass by Earth in 1991.

From the work of NASA scientists, we know without a doubt that space within the solar system is not empty. Many natural orbiting bodies, as well as rings of interplanetary dust, exist in the solar system. A knowledge of the mechanics of orbits gives scientists the power to launch satellites into Earth orbit as well as into orbit around other planets. The data returned from these probes have allowed humanity to learn about Earth and the solar system.

MODELING ELLIPTICAL ORBITS

The path of a body that moves around another object in space is known as an *orbit*. All orbiting objects, be they the planets orbiting the Sun, the many moons in the solar system orbiting their respective planets, or the human-made objects that we have placed into orbit around Earth, obey the same mathematical laws of motion. But we cannot take aerial photographs of orbits as we can of a network of highways or canals, so students may have difficulty conceptualizing orbits, especially when dealing with the scale of distances in space. New graphing technology, however, allows students to model orbits very effectively and, in so doing, to deepen their understanding of the underlying mathematics.

PURPOSES

In this unit, students will learn to model orbits of the Space Station, the Space Shuttle, space probes, the planets, and other satellites. The unit reinforces basic concepts associated with conic sections, and it provides an interesting and important application of the mathematics of the conics. The orbital models involve Cartesian, parametric, and polar graphs. The modeling can be done with whatever graphing utility is available, either a graphing calculator or a computer graphing package.

INTRODUCTION

Throughout history, humans have been fascinated by the motions of the planets, comets, and other celestial bodies. Accounts of their observations and the theories they proposed to explain motion in space fill a rich chapter in the history of mathematical and scientific thought. Two fundamental questions arise from the study of celestial motion: Why do objects orbit? and What paths do orbiting objects follow?

Isaac Newton (1642–1727) answered these questions through his work on universal gravitation. In particular, he explained that the natural path of a planet, for example, is a straight line but that the planet is forced into a curved path by the gravitational pull of the Sun. In his writings, Newton illustrated that a stone projected outward from a point above Earth will, because of gravity, follow a trajectory that pulls it back to Earth (path *a* in fig. 25). If it is projected with greater initial velocity, the stone will travel farther before hitting Earth (paths *b* and *c*). If, however, the initial forward velocity is so fast that the stone's downward trajectory matches the curvature of Earth, then the stone will enter into a circular orbit around Earth (path *d*); and if that initial velocity continues to increase, Earth's curvature will be greater than the trajectory of the stone and an elliptical orbit will result (path *e*). In other words, the orbiting stone is in a state of continually falling toward the center of Earth. If gravity were suddenly to disappear, the stone would fly away in a straight line, just as an object tied to the end of a string and twirled overhead does if the string is suddenly released.

The foregoing description is, of course, greatly simplified. It does not, for example, take into account the effects of Earth's atmosphere, and it gives no indication of the amount of thrust required to achieve orbital velocity. But we are dealing with models, and in modeling we begin with simple, familiar representations and move to more accurate but more complex representations later. Thus, in the earlier units on scaling and on orbital debris, we assumed circular orbits in our models. Now we extend our modeling to the more realistic case of elliptical orbits. In so doing, we revisit some of the considerations of scaling the solar system when we realize the surprisingly close proximity of the satellites that we launch into orbit around Earth.

For these activities, graphing calculators or computer graphing software permits

Curriculum Connections:

Functions

Modeling

Algebra

Trigonometry

Geometry

Related *Mission Mathematics* Activities: *Modeling elliptical orbits is a natural extension of the units on scaling the solar system and modeling orbital-debris problems.*

Fig. 25. Orbital paths around Earth

Ground Control to the crew of Apollo 8: *"Who's driving up there?"*

Apollo 8: *"I think Isaac Newton is doing most of the driving right now."*

Calculators and computers with appropriate software transform the mathematics classroom into a laboratory much like the environment in many science classes, where students use technology to investigate, conjecture, and verify their findings.

(NCTM 1989, p. 128)

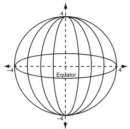

Fig. 26. Cartesian model of Earth

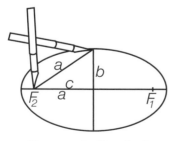

Fig. 27. Finding foci

the focus to be on problem solving, modeling, and exploration. Therefore, the use of a graphing utility is assumed. Although color is not required, it is often available and can enhance classroom presentations. Color is especially appreciated when two orbits are almost identical.

GETTING STARTED

We know that NASA launches satellites into orbit somewhere "up there"—but just where, exactly, is "up there"? This question launches this unit. Students are asked to draw a representation of where they think an orbiting space station might be, relative to Earth.

We expect that the majority of students will sketch a circular or egg-shaped orbit. Many will draw the orbit quite far from the outline of Earth. Some may suggest a static location for the space station rather than an orbit. Unlike images that you may recall from the Apollo missions to the Moon, space station, Shuttle, and satellite orbits are described as Low Earth Orbits (LEOs). The "Aha!" we are leading to in this unit is a rather tight-fitting orbit on a graphing utility. Use this discussion to motivate students to search for a more accurate representation of the Space Station orbit.

THE CARTESIAN MODEL

The development begins with the familiar Cartesian model (fig. 26) in which a circle of radius 4 (from the approximation of 4000 miles for the radius of Earth) is represented by the equation $x^2 + y^2 = 4^2$, or

$$\frac{x^2}{4^2} + \frac{y^2}{4^2} = 1.$$

This latter form promotes the recognition of the circle as a special case of an ellipse. Superimposing ellipses onto a circle representing Earth is presented as a useful technique for producing a three-dimensional effect. You might suggest that students use such a model for Earth when graphing LEOs.

To proceed with the development of this unit, students must be familiar with the mathematics of the ellipse. The student pages include a brief review of basic concepts and of the relationship among the semimajor axis, a, the semiminor axis, b, and the center-focus distance, c: $a^2 = b^2 + c^2$. In the student pages, this relationship is called the "a, b, c connection." The student pages also present the pins-and-string method of constructing ellipses, and we encourage you to have your students explore that construction to get an intuitive sense of how the shape of the ellipse depends on the separation of the two foci. This exploration will lead naturally to the definition of the *eccentricity* of an ellipse: $e = c/a$.

Find My Focus

Students enjoy the ellipse game "find my focus" in which they are given an unmarked ellipse and are challenged to find its two foci. Although many ways are possible to produce ellipses for this game, including the string construction—although you must be careful not to have any pin holes showing—perhaps the easiest and quickest way is to use a computer drawing program. Almost all drawing and painting programs include an ellipse tool with which you can draw ellipses of any desired size or shape in a matter of seconds.

Emphasize to your students that you are interested not so much in the location of the foci of a particular ellipse as you are in a strategy for finding them. One solution that students may suggest is the following (fig. 27):

1. Locate the major and minor axes on the ellipse, perhaps by folding the paper.

2. Set a compass to the length of the semimajor axis, *a*.

3. Place the compass point where the minor axis intersects the ellipse.

4. Swing the pencil end of the compass to mark two intersections with the major axis. These are the foci of the ellipse, each at a distance c from the center of the ellipse.

Eccentricity

Eccentricity, e, is a "pure number" without dimension. Moving the pins in the string construction enhances students' understanding of e. If you separate the pins so wide that the pencil runs along the major axis, you will illustrate the extreme case in which $c = a$ and the "ellipse" degenerates into a line segment. At the other extreme, you can move the pins closer and closer together until you use only one pin. Now $c = 0$, and your trace is a circle. Between these two extremes, you will construct ellipses of various degrees of elongation.

Modeling the Orbit of the Space Station

To understand what we are attempting to do in the problems that follow, students must be familiar with Kepler's first law: An object in orbit around another body moves in an elliptical path with the body at one focus of the ellipse. In the context that we present here, the Space Station moves in an elliptical path with the center of Earth at one focus.

The first attempt to model the orbit of the Space Station uses Cartesian coordinates and introduces two important but probably unfamiliar terms: *apogee,* the

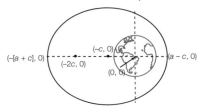

point on the orbit farthest from Earth, and *perigee,* the point on the orbit closest to Earth. What is likely to be the most difficult initial task for the students is placing the coordinates so that the origin of the coordinate system coincides with the center of Earth at one focus of the orbit. Relevant coordinates in this system are shown in figure 28.

Fig. 28. Origin of coordinate system coincides with center of Earth at one focus.

Extension: *Students should be encouraged to read some of the many accounts of the work of Kepler and Newton. Of particular significance is the connection between Kepler's laws, which were derived empirically from data, and Newton's subsequent theoretical verification of Kepler's conclusions.*

Athough Kepler's first law is the only one of his three laws mentioned in this activity, the mathematics of the other two also leads to rich investigations. See, for example, the student pages in the scaling unit.

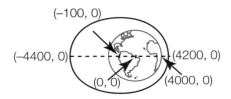

Fig. 29. Coordinates of desired points

Solutions: ✔ Your Understanding

It is not possible to represent Earth and the orbit to scale and still show the coordinates of the desired points; hence, the diagram in figure 29 is badly out of scale.

1. The major axis = $2a$ = 400 + 4000 + 4000 + 200 = 8600 miles; $a = 4300$ miles. To calculate c, the "shift" distance from (0, 0), locate the midpoint of the major axis and note that c is 100 miles "left" of (0, 0). Thus, $c = 100$ miles. Knowing a and c, we can calculate b with the "a, b, c connection."

$$b = \sqrt{a^2 - c^2} = 4298.8$$

Finally, $e = c/a = 100/4300 = 0.0232558$.

2. One form of the equation is

$$\frac{(x + 0.1)^2}{4.3^2} + \frac{y^2}{\left(\sqrt{4.3^2 - 0.1^2}\right)^2} = 1,$$

when we use a scale of 1 unit = 1000 miles.

3. The graph should show a very tight-fitting orbit around Earth, similar to the illustration in figure 30a. Figure 30b shows a screen print of the same orbit.

4. Apogee and perigee distances are 4400 miles and 4200 miles, respectively.

6. We anticipate surprise at the tight fit of the orbit. If we represent Earth with an orange, then the distance from the fruit to the skin is a good visualization for tight-fitting low Earth orbits.

(a)
A tight-fitting orbit around Earth

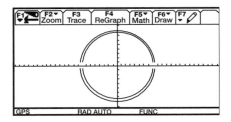

(b)
Screen print from a graphing utility

Fig. 30

THE PARAMETRIC MODEL

The limitations of a Cartesian model set the stage for a parametric model of orbits in which we introduce *t*, the parameter, as a measure of rotation. In orbital mechanics, *t* is known as the *true anomaly*. It measures the angle between a line connecting the center of Earth to the perigee point and a line (the radius) connecting the center of Earth to the satellite's current position. This angle is illustrated on student page 76. The parametric method is introduced with the circle; the trigonometry should be familiar to students.

t	*x*	*y*
0°	*4*	*0*
45°	*2.8*	*2.8*
60°	*2*	*3.5*
90°	*0*	*4*

Fig. 31. Examples of parametric values

If graphing with parametric equations is new to your students, you may want to begin with some basic hands-on parametric graphing. For example, have students graph our Earth model as a circle with radius = 4. The parametric representation is $x = r\cos(t)$ and $y = r\sin(t)$, where $r = 4$. You may want students to plot, by hand, some ordered triples to observe that the graph is a circle (fig. 31). Decide on either degree or radian mode for the rotation *t*. Students should set their graphing utility to the parametric mode and plot several circles.

Assessment Tip: ***Ask students to demonstrate their understanding by showing you the orbital plots on their graphing utilities.***

Graphing the ellipse in the parametric mode is then developed as an extension of graphing circles. Once again, the center of the coordinate system is placed at the focus of the ellipse (the center of Earth), so the resulting parametric equations for the ellipse are $x = a\cos(t) - c$ and $y = b\sin(t)$. As before, students should verify the model with many plots on a graphing utility.

We then return to graphing the LEO of the space station. Here we use the values calculated previously: $a = 4.3$, $c = 0.1$, and $b = \sqrt{a^2 - c^2}$, where we let 1 unit = 1000 miles. We also prefer to express *b* in terms of *a* and *c* rather than deal with the decimal approximation.

When we plot the orbit on our graphing utility and do a trace, the space station moves through the exact apogee and perigee given in the specifications. We expect students to comment on how "complete" the orbit is now compared with the Cartesian plots. No gaps will appear near the *x*-axis, and students should also note how well the trace models the actual movement of the space station around Earth.

Students who are able to apply and translate among different representations of the same problem situation or the same mathematical concept will have at once a powerful, flexible set of tools for solving problems and a deeper appreciation of the consistency and beauty of mathematics.

(NCTM 1989, p. 146)

THE POLAR MODEL

The third model we introduce is the polar model, which is commonly used in navigation. If you have pilot experience or have any pilots in class, you may want to elaborate on this connection. What may at first appear to be a "problem," the multiple representations for the same point in polar coordinates, actually becomes an advantage in modeling the position of spacecraft. This will be illustrated in some of the activities later in the unit.

The connection between Cartesian and polar models is shown below:

Cartesian	Polar
$y = 5$	$R(t)\sin(t) = 5$ or $R(t) = 5/\sin(t) = 5\csc(t)$
$x = 2$	$R\cos(t) = 2$
$y^2 = 4x$	$R(t) = 4\cos(t)\csc^2(t)$
$\frac{x^2}{9} + \frac{y^2}{4} = 1$	$R(t) = \frac{6}{\sqrt{4\cos^2(t) + 9\sin^2(t)}}$

Teaching Tip: ***In this unit we use*** e ***to represent eccentricity. Be sure to check your graphing utility to see if it interprets*** e ***to mean Euler's constant. If it does, use another letter to represent eccentricity.***

The last entry is the equation of an ellipse with semimajor axis = 3 and semiminor axis = 2. It is used to show how the polar form can be transformed into a more useful model,

$$R(t) = \frac{a(1 - e^2)}{1 + e\cos(t)},$$

where a is the semimajor axis, e is the eccentricity, and the parameter t is the true anomaly.

To arrive at this equation, it is first necessary to introduce the classic focus-directrix definition of conic sections, which you may want to review with your students:

> The path of a point in the plane whose distance, d, from a fixed point (the *focus*) has a constant ratio to its distance from a fixed line (the *directrix*) is a conic. The constant ratio e is the eccentricity of the conic. If $e > 1$, the conic is a hyperbola; if $e = 1$, the conic is a parabola; if $0 < e < 1$, the conic is an ellipse.

That definition leads to the equation

$$R = R(t) = \frac{ed}{1 + e \cos(t)},$$

which is derived in the student pages. It has the advantage of being applicable to all conic sections, depending on the value of e as noted. Once again, students are encouraged to explore the meaning of this equation with their graphing utilities, paying particular attention to what happens to the graph as they change the values of e and d.

A rich extension of this activity can be developed by plotting the orbits of comets on a graphing utility. Values for the orbital elements of some comets can be found in astronomy books and at several Internet locations. Three examples follow in table 9.

Technology Tip: *Dynamic geometry software provides an effective medium for students to explore the focus-directrix relationships in conics.*

Teaching Tip: *Compare the eccentricities of these comet orbits with the planetary eccentricities given in the scaling unit.*

Table 9
Values for Orbital Elements of Three Comets

Comet	Eccentricity	Perihelion (in astronomical units)
Hyakutake	0.9997	0.2301957
Szczepanski	close to 1	1.4507841
Jedicke	0.3950995	4.1365894

Extension: *In the comet data, we have ignored the inclination of the orbits. The orbit of comet Hyakutake (1996), for example, was tilted at a steep angle of nearly 125 degrees. Students may want to pursue adding this parameter to their models.*

In table 9, *perihelion* is the minimum distance of the comet from the Sun, analogous to perigee in orbits around Earth. Perihelion is given in astronomical units (AU), where one AU is the distance of Earth from the Sun, approximately 93 000 000 miles. The semimajor axis, a, can be calculated using the relationship $H_p = (a - c) = (a - a \cdot e) = a(1 - e)$. Students will gain an appreciation of the profound effect that a small change in the eccentricity has on the orbit. They should also compare the orbits of comets, with their large eccentricities, with the planetary orbits whose eccentricities can be found in the scaling unit.

Applying the Polar Model

To illustrate the usefulness of the polar model, which may not be immediately apparent, students are asked to use the polar form to graph the space station orbit from the earlier problems as well as the orbit of a Space Shuttle mission, STS-73, which flew in October 1995. Note that the altitudes of apogee and perigee for the Shuttle orbit are given in nautical miles. Students will need the conversion factor 1 nautical mile = 1.151 statute miles. This is also a good time to engage students in discussion about the number of significant figures that they can reasonably use and their effect on the precision of the plots.

Teaching Tip: *You can make this activity even more timely by graphing the orbit of the most recent Shuttle mission. The Shuttle page on NASA's World Wide Web site presents data about the flights, including the orbital elements. Students can check the NASA site and select the mission that they wish to model.*

Modeling a Rendezvous

Here we come to the most important element in our study of orbits: how to change an orbit while in space. Changing orbits is accomplished by firing small rocket engines called *thrusters* to effect a change in speed, direction, or both.

Connections: *At this point you may want to include a detailed presentation of change in velocity and vectors, although we do not take that approach here. You also may want to refer students to Newton's laws of motion for insight into why the thruster rockets are fired in the opposite direction of the desired velocity change.*

When the thruster is fired, the change in the spacecraft's velocity occurs in the *opposite* direction. Thus, to increase the forward motion of the spacecraft, the rocket is fired in the reverse direction, which is known as a *posigrade burn*. A *retrograde burn* fires the thruster in the forward direction, causing the spacecraft to decrease its forward velocity. For simplicity, we assume that the thruster burn occurs instantaneously, although in reality the burn takes seconds or even minutes. This assumption of instantaneous burn leads to an important principle of orbital flight: The point at which the burn occurs is a point on both the original and the new orbits. In other words, the burn changes every point on the new orbit except the burn point.

The problem presented in the student pages involves a rendezvous with the Hubble Space Telescope. In the initial orbit, H_p = 200 miles and H_a = 400 miles; in the desired orbit, H_a = 800 miles and the burn occurs at perigee—hence, H_p remains 200 miles. Orbital elements for the two orbits are as follows:

	Initial Orbit	Final Orbit
a	4300 miles	4500 miles
c	100 miles	300 miles
e	100/4300 = 0.02326	300/4500 = 0.06667
Perigee	(4200, 0°)	(4200, 0°)
Apogee	(4400, 180°)	(4800, 180°)

Facility with mathematical language and notation enables students to more easily form multiple representations of ideas, express relationships within and among representational systems, and formulate generalizations.

(NCTM 1989, p. 140)

The problem posed "for experts only" is a reality check for our modeling. If done properly, the trace will move in the initial orbit for three revolutions, then simulate the burn and change to the final orbital path. One way to represent this orbit with a polar model follows:

$$R(t) = \begin{cases} \dfrac{4300\left(1-\left(\dfrac{100}{4300}\right)^2\right)}{1+\left(\dfrac{100}{4300}\right)\cos(t)}, & 0 \le t < 3\cdot 360° \end{cases}$$

$$R(t) = \begin{cases} \dfrac{4500\left(1-\left(\dfrac{300}{4500}\right)^2\right)}{1+\left(\dfrac{300}{4500}\right)\cos(t)}, & 3\cdot 360° \le t \le 8\cdot 360° \end{cases}$$

Students experience a real sense of accomplishment when their traces actually model the mission. The orbits plotted on a graphing utility will resemble the screen print in figure 32:

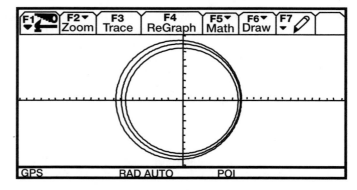

Fig. 32. Screen print from a graphing utility

Pick Your Project

At this point students should be ready for "full space simulation" on their graphing utilities, so we conclude the unit with five activities and encourage students to choose from among them or design their own modeling investigations.

Eccentric … or Not?

A polar plot of this orbit should look something like the graph in figure 33a or the screen print in figure 33b. It is not hard to argue that the television analyst was wrong about the eccentricity. Note that this orbit is the same one that we used in the earlier Hubble rendezvous problem, in which we calculated the eccentricity to be 0.06667. (This activity is adapted from an example in *To Rise from Earth* by Wayne Lee, Texas Space Grant Consortium, 1994, p. 32.)

Modeling the Rendezvous with Mir

This activity is a variation on the Hubble rendezvous activity presented earlier. Different graphing utilities will present different options for the small-window (zoom) investigation.

Modeling the Orbit of the Moon

After studying many examples of LEOs, students may be surprised to observe the difference between the tight-fitting orbits of spacecraft and the lunar orbit, and they should arrive at a new appreciation of the Apollo missions. The scale of the window will be essential for this model. To represent the orbit of the Moon in the graphing-utility window, Earth is likely to appear as a single pixel hardly visible on the screen.

Exploring the Solar System

This activity is a natural extension of the models of the solar system developed in the scaling unit where, for simplicity, we assumed circular orbits. Here students can plot the elliptical orbits of the planets using the data on planetary distances and eccentricities of the orbits. After plotting these orbits, students should be asked to evaluate the appropriateness of our earlier assumption of circular orbits.

We have found that a window of [–2, 2] by [–2, 2] is convenient for the four inner planets and that the minimum number of windows to best display the solar system on a graphing utility is two. A second window [–50, 50] by [–50, 50] gives a nice display of the outer planets.

For Experts Only!

Students who have mastered the technique of modeling orbits on their graphing utilities are challenged to extend their study by investigating how to plot orbits that are inclined to the equatorial plane of Earth. This question is left as an open-ended challenge for both students and teachers.

Experiences designed to foster continued intellectual curiosity and increasing independence should encourage students to become self-directed learners who routinely engage in constructing, symbolizing, applying, and generalizing mathematical ideas.

(NCTM 1989, p. 128)

(a)
Tight-fitting orbit

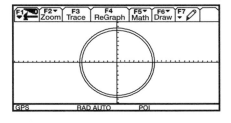

(b)
Screen print from a graphing utility
Fig. 33

Related *Mission Mathematics* Activities: *This project is a natural extension of the modeling activities in the "Scaling the Heights" unit.*

It's your graduation night. Television cameras focus on your face. The reporter asks, "So what are you going to do now?" You answer, "I'm going to Disney World!"

Fast-forward to the year 2000. Again you are in the glare of television lights. "So what are you going to do now?" This time your reply is, "I'm going to the space station!"

Orlando is on your map, but where is the space station—*exactly?* In the box below, illustrate where you think the Space Station is. Compare your drawing with those of other students. Discuss similarities and differences in your sketches. Listen for words that best describe how to locate the space station.

In this unit you will learn to model orbits of the space station, the Space Shuttle, space probes, the planets, and other satellites. Essential information for modeling will be found in many forms:

◆ Symbolic: equations, formulas, written "laws"

◆ Numeric: tables, spreadsheets, flight data, charts

◆ Graphic: sketches, Cartesian graphs, polar graphs

◆ Scenic: observing an event firsthand or from a written account, a movie, a television program, a video, a simulation, or a World Wide Web site

Modeling always produces a healthy tension between *accuracy* and *simplicity:* a simple model is often not very accurate, and a precise model is seldom simple. These are the dynamics of modeling. So we begin with simple models and progress to more accurate representations, but as with all interesting applications of mathematics, the journey is open-ended. We urge you to continue the mission as far as your curiosity and enthusiasm take you.

The countdown begins.

MODELING ORBITS WITH A GRAPHING UTILITY

STAGE ONE: CARTESIAN COORDINATES

Suppose that you want a more accurate sketch to observe the orbit of the space station around Earth. Several ways are available to use your graphing utility (graphing calculator or computer graphics program) for these observations. We'll begin with the familiar Cartesian coordinate system.

Graph an outline of Earth by assuming a circular profile with Earth's radius of 4000 miles (6000 kilometers). Try a [−5000, 5000] by [−5000, 5000] window or a window of [−5, 5] by [−5, 5] where each unit stands for 1000 miles. Recall the Cartesian equation for a circle with radius 4 units:

$$x^2 + y^2 = 4^2$$

or

$$\frac{x^2}{4^2} + \frac{y^2}{4^2} = 1$$

You can get a simple three-dimensional effect by superimposing ellipses of the equator and some longitudinal lines as shown here. We shall return shortly to exact instructions for creating this simulation of the globe. First, however, let's review what you know about ellipses.

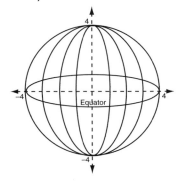

The Ellipse: A Review

The standard form for the equation of an ellipse centered at (h, k) in the Cartesian plane, with semimajor axis equal to a

and semiminor axis equal to b is

$$\frac{(x-h)^2}{a^2} + \frac{(y-k)^2}{b^2} = 1.$$

When the center is at the origin, the equation becomes

$$\frac{x^2}{a^2} + \frac{y^2}{b^2} = 1.$$

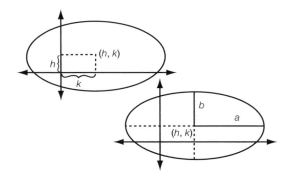

Recall the locus definition of this conic: a set of points in the plane such that the sum of the distances from two fixed points, called *foci*, remains constant. One way to sketch an ellipse using string and two pins is shown below. We can use this device to reveal meaningful relationships among the essential elements a (the *semimajor axis*), b (the *semiminor axis*), and c (the *center-focus distance*) of the ellipse.

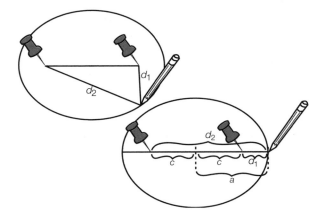

To draw an ellipse, use your pencil to stretch a string around two pushpins as shown. Because the length of the string does not change, the distances d_1 and d_2 have a constant sum; therefore, the path traced by your pencil will be an ellipse with foci at F_1 and F_2, the locations of the pins. We shall represent the sum as $d_1 + d_2 = k$.

To determine the value of k, move your pencil to one end of the major axis (see the figure). We can see that $d_1 = a - c$ and $d_2 = a + c$. So $d_1 + d_2 = 2a$; thus, $k = 2a$. Further, this constant sum, $2a$, is the length of the major axis.

The "A, B, C Connection"

Position your pencil on the endpoint of the minor axis as shown. Now the string triangle is isosceles, and the two pencil-to-pin distances are equal. We know the sum of the distances is $2a$, so each distance equals a. Use the right-triangle relationship to find an equation that involves a, b, and c. Write your equation in the box:

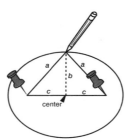

The "a, b, c connection"

Ellipse Game: Find My Foci

To play the game called "find my foci," draw an accurate ellipse using the string method, a graphing utility, a template, or any other precise method. Be sure that the foci are not visible when you show the ellipse to another player. The object of the game is to locate precisely both foci of the ellipse. Play the game several times and describe a strategy for finding the foci.

Eccentricity

If you play long enough with the string construction of ellipses, you will notice how the shapes change as you move the

foci—the pins—closer together and farther apart. The amount of deviation from the circle is called the *eccentricity* of the ellipse and is defined by the ratio c/a. The extremes for this ratio are 0 and 1. Therefore, for any ellipse $0 < c/a < 1$ or $0 < e < 1$, where e stands for *eccentricity*. Although the letter e is often used in print for eccentricity, be careful using it with your calculator or graphing device, which may interpret e as Euler's constant: $2.718281828459045...$—approximately.

Take a close look at the ellipse for the extreme values of e: What kind of an ellipse do you get if e equals 0? How does the ellipse look when e equals 1?

Constructing a 3-D Model of Earth

We return to the construction of a three-dimensional model of Earth with a graphing utility. With the suggested window of $[-5, 5]$ by $[-5, 5]$, where each unit stands for 1000 miles, superimpose the following ellipses, all with centers at $(0, 0)$:

$$
\begin{array}{ll}
a = 4, b = 4 & \text{(Earth outline)} \\
a = 4, b = 1 & \text{(equator)} \\
a = 3, b = 4 \\
a = 2, b = 4 & \text{(lines of longitude)} \\
a = 1, b = 4
\end{array}
$$

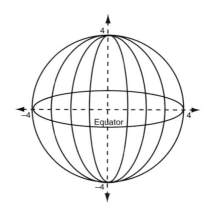

MODELING THE ORBIT OF THE SPACE STATION ON A GRAPHING UTILITY

Ever since the brilliant analysis by Johannes Kepler (1571–1630), we have known that all planets, moons, double stars, and human-made satellites obey certain very precise laws as they move through the cosmos. Kepler's first law states the following:

> A planet moves in an ellipse with the Sun at one of the two foci.

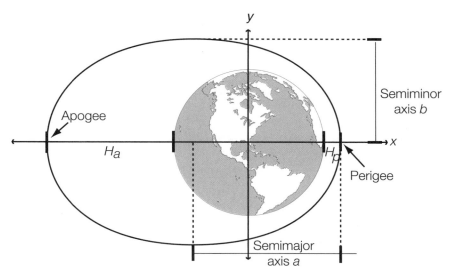

Applied to our space-station orbit, it reads this way:

> A space station moves in an ellipse with the center of Earth at one of the two foci.

The Cartesian Model

To help see the *a, b, c* connection for this context, we look at a sketch (badly out of scale) for such an orbit. Note that the center of Earth is at one focus of the ellipse. We also introduce two new terms: *apogee,* the point on the orbit farthest from Earth, and *perigee,* the point on the orbit closest to Earth. In the diagram, H_a equals the altitude of apogee and H_p equals the altitude of perigee. For our first model, let's assume that NASA expects the altitude of apogee to be 400 miles and the altitude of perigee to be 200 miles.

✔ Your Understanding:

1. Use these data, $H_a = 400$ and $H_p = 200$, and the 4000-mile radius of Earth to find—

   a, the length of the semimajor axis;
   b, the length of the semiminor axis;

   c, the center-focus distance;
   e, the eccentricity of the orbit.

2. Write a Cartesian equation for the elliptical orbit.

3. Use your graphing utility to graph a model of Earth. Superimpose the elliptical orbit on your graph of Earth.

4. Locate the points of apogee and perigee on your graph, and verify that your plot conforms to the NASA specifications.

5. Do a trace on your graphing utility to simulate the movement of the space station in orbit.

6. As you look at your model of the orbit on your graphing utility, are you surprised by any aspect of the image? Suppose that Earth is represented by an orange. How would you describe the distance of the space-station orbit from the orange? Write a paragraph to summarize what you observe. Include any surprises or unexpected results you experienced as you completed this model of the orbit.

The Parametric Model

Some aspects of a Cartesian model for orbits are clumsy and not realistic. For example, the trace does not model the movement of the space station very well. You also may notice a gap in the plot (pixels) near the semimajor axis. This gap is the result of "pixelitis"—the problems in using a finite device (your graphing utility) to approximate a continuous function. You can improve the graph on some devices by plotting more points, but the Cartesian model will always be flawed near the x-axis. For these and other reasons that will soon be apparent, astronomers and NASA scientists use other models to represent orbits.

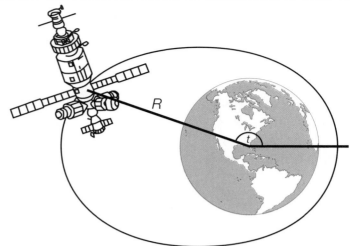

The parametric model uses the radius R, which is the distance between the satellite (the space station) and Earth, and an angle (θ or t) called the *true anomaly*. True anomaly measures the angle between a line connecting the center of Earth to the perigee point and a line (the radius) connecting the center of Earth to the satellite's position. In our development here, we use t to represent the true anomaly.

You may recall how to graph circles using a parametric method. With basic trigonometry, it is easy to show that the Cartesian coordinates (x, y) for any point on a circle with radius r can be represented using the parameter t as follows:

$$x = r\cos(t)$$

and

$$y = r\sin(t)$$

These equations are parametric equations for a circle with center at $(0, 0)$ and radius r. For an ellipse centered at $(0, 0)$ with semimajor axis a

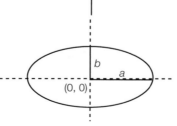

and semiminor axis b, the Cartesian equation is

$$\frac{x^2}{a^2} + \frac{y^2}{b^2} = 1.$$

Parametric equations for this ellipse are $x = a\cos(t)$ and $y = b\sin(t)$. You can verify this result on your graphing utility or symbolically, as shown below, by employing a classic identity to eliminate the parameter t.

$$\cos(t) = x/a \qquad \sin(t) = y/b$$
$$\cos^2(t) = x^2/a^2 \qquad \sin^2(t) = y^2/b^2$$
$$\cos^2(t) + \sin^2(t) = 1$$
$$\frac{x^2}{a^2} + \frac{y^2}{b^2} = 1$$

But in the case of a body in orbit around Earth, the center of the elliptical orbit is at $(-c, 0)$, not at $(0, 0)$. Thus the x-coordinate of our parametric equation is translated by the amount $-c$. The resulting equations are $x = a\cos(t) - c$ and $y = b\sin(t)$.

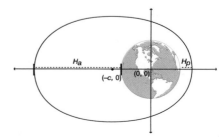

✔ Your Understanding:

1. Set your graphing utility in the parametric mode and verify that the parametric equations $x = r\cos(t)$ and $y = r\sin(t)$ will produce circles for various values of r.

2. Use the equations $x = a\cos(t) - c$ and $y = b\sin(t)$ to graph a parametric model for the orbit of the space station when $H_a = 400$ miles and $H_p = 200$ miles.

3. Do a trace to simulate the movement of the space station in orbit, and verify the coordinates at points of apogee and perigee. How do they compare with NASA's specifications?

4. Write a report to explain possible advantages of this parametric model over the Cartesian model for Low Earth Orbits on a graphing utility.

The Polar Model

A convenient way to locate aircraft is similar to using polar coordinates. The distance, R, from the tower to the aircraft is a function of the angle t. The connection between this (R, t) polar location and the (x, y) Cartesian location is clear from the right-triangle trigonometry:

$$x/R = \cos(t) \quad x = R\cos(t) \quad R = \sqrt{x^2 + y^2}$$
$$y/R = \sin(t) \quad y = R\sin(t) \quad \tan(t) = y/x$$

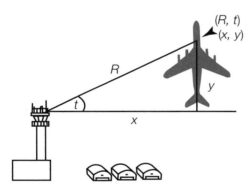

It is important to note that although the Cartesian coordinates for a given point are unique, an infinite number of polar-coordinate representations for the same point are possible. For example, the point with Cartesian coordinates $(1,1)$ can have the following polar coordinates:

$$\left(\sqrt{2}, 45°\right), \left(\sqrt{2}, 405°\right), \left(\sqrt{2}, 765°\right), ...,$$
$$\left(\sqrt{2}, 45° + (n) \cdot 360°\right)$$

where $n = 0, 1, 2, ...$.

This information can be useful when we want to model spacecraft that remain in one elliptical orbit for several days before executing a retrograde burn to move into another orbit.

You can gain an intuitive appreciation of polar-coordinate graphing in many ways:

- Your graphing utility may have excellent built-in software to display simultaneous polar and Cartesian graphs.

- Your local television weather radar can be a great visual tool if the sweep of the radar is shown.

- Playing with such toys as the Spirograph can promote an understanding of complex polar graphs.

- A study of microphone sensitivity plots will reveal a nice application of polar graphing.

- Visit a local radio station and ask an engineer to show you the antenna patterns, which are polar charts that the station must file with the Federal Communications Commission (FCC).

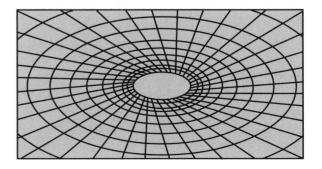

Connecting the Models

To further examine the connection between the Cartesian and polar models, consider the two ways of representing a circle:

Cartesian	Polar
$x^2 + y^2 = 4^2$	$R = 4$ or $R(t) = 4$

Complete the table below using the equations given on the previous page. Then plot the graphs in both polar and Cartesian coordinates to verify your work.

Cartesian	Polar
$y = 5$	$R(t) \cdot \sin(t) = 5$ $R(t) = 5/\sin(t) = 5\csc(t)$
	$R \cdot \cos(t) = 2$
$y^2 = 4x$	
$\dfrac{x^2}{9} + \dfrac{y^2}{4} = 1$	

The connection between polar and parametric forms can also be derived from the equations on the previous page. Here we use the fact that $x = R \cos(t)$ and $y = R \sin(t)$, and we make the "R replacement." For example,

if the polar form is

$$R = R(t) = 6 \tan(t),$$

then the parametric form is

$$x = R \cos(t) = R(t) \cos(t) = [6 \tan(t)]\cos(t)$$

$$y = R \sin(t) = R(t) \sin(t) = [6 \tan(t)]\sin(t).$$

You should verify several similar plots before you proceed. If your graphing utility does not include polar coordinates, you can use the parametric representation to produce a polar-coordinate graph.

Polar-Coordinate Model for Any Ellipse

The last entry in the foregoing table is an ellipse with semimajor axis equal to 3 and semiminor axis equal to 2. Your polar equation should look something like the following:

$$R = R(t) = \frac{6}{\sqrt{4\cos^2(t) + 9\sin^2(t)}}$$

We could continue to use this type of polar equation for the ellipse. However, it is possible to derive a much more useful model. For space science and astronomy, the most useful model is a polar-coordinate model,

$$R(t) = \frac{a\left(1 - e^2\right)}{1 + e \cos(t)},$$

where a is the semimajor axis, $e = c/a$ is the eccentricity, and t is the true-anomaly angle.

The derivation of this model is nice mathematics that depends on a second useful definition of eccentricity. Up to this point we have defined eccentricity only as it applies to the shape of an ellipse. This second definition involves the classic *focus-directrix* definition of conic sections. The equation we derive subsequently yields a model for plotting any conic on a graphing utility. Therefore, it can be used to model suborbital flight and parabolic or hyperbolic flyby trajectories as well as orbital paths.

The Focus-Directrix Polar Model

Cartesian models for conics—ellipses, parabolas, and hyperbolas—are simple when the origin lies at the center of the conic. But in modeling orbits, it is more convenient to place a focus at the reference point or origin. Polar models of conics have the advantage of taking a simple form if one of the foci lies at the point $(R, t) = (0, 0)$. This point is called the *pole* in polar coordinates; it corresponds to the origin in the Cartesian plane.

The focus-directrix definition of eccentricity provides a means to classify all conic sections:

The path of a point in the plane whose distance from a fixed point, the *focus,* has a constant ratio to its distance from a fixed line, the *directrix,* is a conic. The constant ratio *e* is the eccentricity of the conic. If $e > 1$, the conic is a hyperbola; if $e = 1$, the conic is a parabola, and if $0 < e < 1$, the conic is an ellipse.

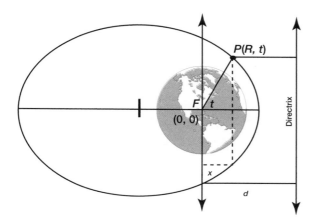

In this polar graph, the focus *F* is located at the pole (0, 0). *P* is any point on the conic with coordinates (*R*, *t*). The directrix is located at a distance *d* from the focus. We want to show that the polar equation of any conic is

$$R = R(t) = \frac{ed}{1+e\cos(t)}. \qquad (1)$$

The constant ratio is

$$e = \frac{|PF|}{|PD|}$$

where $|PF| = R$ and $|PD| = d - x$. But $x/R = \cos(t)$, so $x = R\cos(t)$ and we have $|PD| = d - R\cos(t)$. Thus,

$$e = \frac{R}{d - R\cos(t)}.$$

Solving for *R* yields the desired equation (1).

✔ **Your Understanding:**
1. Enter the polar equation for conics,

$$R = R(t) = \frac{ed}{1+e\cos(t)},$$

into your graphing utility. Keep the focus-directrix distance constant (let $d = 1$, for example) and change the value of *e*, the eccentricity. Verify the claim that the value of *e* determines whether the graph is a hyperbola, parabola, or ellipse.

2. Write a report of your study. Explain what to expect from changing the value of *e*.

3. Complete a similar study holding *e* constant and changing the value of *d* for at least one conic.

4. Write a report to explain how we might apply hyperbolic, parabolic, and elliptical paths to space flight or to comets.

The Polar Model for Elliptical Orbits

Remember the polar model for an ellipse that we earlier "pulled out of a hat"? Here it is again:

$$R(t) = \frac{a(1-e^2)}{1+e\cos(t)}.$$

Can we show that the polar model for conics,

$$R = R(t) = \frac{ed}{1+e\cos(t)},$$

yields this equation for an ellipse?

Consider any ellipse with semimajor axis *a*, focus at (0, 0), directrix *d* units right of the focus, and eccentricity *e*, as shown in the figure on the next page. Here $|PF| = a - c$ and $e = c/a$, so $c = a \cdot e$. Then

$$|PF| = a - ae = a(1 - e).$$

But because $|PF| = R(t)$ when $t = 0$ and $\cos(0) = 1$, the polar equation becomes

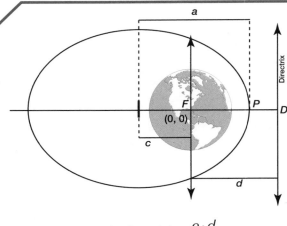

$$|PF| = R(0) = \frac{e \cdot d}{1+e}.$$

These two expressions for |PF| give the following:

$$\frac{ed}{1+e} = a(1-e),$$
$$ed = a(1-e)(1+e),$$

or

$$e \cdot d = a(1-e^2)$$

We've got it! For the ellipse with focus at (0, 0), the two equations are equivalent.

APPLYING THE POLAR MODEL: YOUR GRAPHING UTILITY AS A SPACE NAVIGATOR

At this point you may still wonder why we have identified the polar model as the most useful. Given only apogee-perigee data, we find that other models are certainly easy to use. However, space scientists and astronomers often use the *orbital elements* or *Keplerian elements, a* and *e.* In fact, if you access the NASA shuttle page on the World Wide Web during a mission, the first two Keplerian elements listed will be *a* and *e.* The following activities illustrate how the polar equations and your graphing utility can be used to model Low Earth Orbits (LEO).

But first a cautionary message from Mission Control: Before you enter the polar model in your graphing utility, be alert for anomalies.

(*a*) Check when entering the eccentricity, *e,* to be sure that it is not interpreted as Euler's constant, 2.718…. If it is, use another letter for eccentricity.

(*b*) Check the angle setting for *t* (or theta), the true anomaly, to see if it is in radians or degrees. For a complete elliptical orbit, $0 < t < 2\pi$ or $0 < t < 360°$. You may want to try modeling in both modes before you decide on your setting.

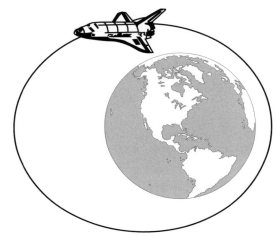

Modeling Low Earth Orbits

1. As a preflight check, graph the space station orbit again, using the polar model. Recall the specifications: perigee at 200 miles and apogee at 400 miles. Compute *a* and *e.* Graph the orbit on your graphing utility, and do a trace to check it.

2. Keplerian elements for a recent NASA Space Shuttle mission (STS-73, October 1995) were *a* = 6 644 100.18 meters and *e* = 0.0002952. Superimpose this orbit on an outline of Earth on your graphing utility. Because the NASA data are so precise, you may want to use 3960 miles for the radius of Earth.

Note that you will need to convert a to miles or Earth's radius to meters.

3. NASA's World Wide Web page for that mission also listed the altitudes at apogee and perigee: $H_a = 144.658$ nautical miles and $H_p = 142.540$ nautical miles. Prepare a report on your graphing project. Include a discussion on the accuracy of your orbit plot. How many significant digits did you use in operations with the data? Did that have an effect on the accuracy of your plot?

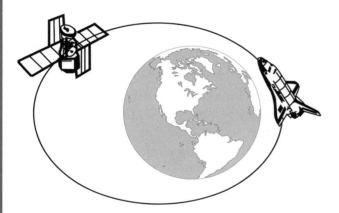

Modeling a Rendezvous with the Hubble Space Telescope

Assume that you are in orbit with the Space Shuttle. For ease in calculating, let's say that your altitudes of perigee and apogee are the same as they were for the space station orbit: 200 miles and 400 miles, respectively. You are in the second orbit of your mission when you receive this transmission from Mission Control:

"This is Houston…We have a problem with the Hubble Space Telescope that needs your attention. Please prepare for a posigrade burn to change your orbit and rendezvous with the Hubble. Apogee for the Hubble orbit is 800 miles."

Assume that the burn will take place at perigee in your orbit. The burn point will become perigee of your new orbit also because the burn raises every point on the old orbit except the burn point.

1. Plot Earth on your graphing utility with $r = 4000$ miles.

2. Superimpose your Shuttle orbit on the outline of Earth. You should be able to calculate a and c from the data given; use your polar model and recall that $e = c/a$.

3. With the information from Houston, calculate the orbital elements for your new orbit. It must have a perigee of 200 miles and an apogee of 800 miles.

4. Use your polar model to superimpose the new orbit on the plot from step 2.

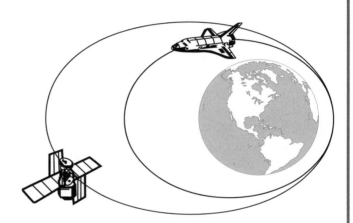

For Experts Only

Modify your work for plotting the two orbits in such a way that a trace of your polar model on your graphing utility will remain in the initial orbit (perigee 200 miles, apogee 400 miles) for three complete orbits. Then, simulating the burn at perigee, the trace will move into the new orbit (perigee 200 miles, apogee 800 miles) for five complete orbits. (Hint: Pay close attention to the "a, c, e connections" and recall how to define a function that changes over different parts of its domain. In this example, we have two parts to the domain for t.)

Pick Your Project

Mission Control reports that all systems are "go" for modeling in space. Your graphing utility is a space simulator that

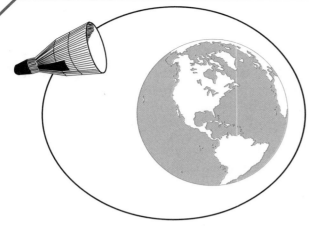

can transport you instantly into the cosmos. You can travel to the Shuttle, to the Moon, to Mars and Jupiter, to any destination in the galaxy and beyond. Just pick your mission from the activities that follow, or design your own unique investigation of space. If your graphing utility has three-dimensional capability, the possibilities are more intriguing. When a NASA mission is in progress, the drama unfolds on NASA-TV, and the World Wide Web becomes a rich source of immediate data and images to fuel your investigation. Enjoy the journey!

✦ Eccentric … or Not?

In the mid-1960s, U.S. astronauts flew on a mission that used an orbit with a perigee altitude of 200 miles and an apogee altitude of 800 miles. A television analyst covering the mission commented, "Wow, what an eccentric orbit!"

At first glance, that orbit seemed very eccentric, with apogee four times the distance of perigee. However, the analyst failed to recall that orbital calculations depend primarily on the radius r, the distance of the spacecraft from the center of Earth. Evaluate the reporter's claim by doing the following:

- Approximate the radius of Earth as 4000 miles and compare the values of r at apogee and perigee.

- Compute the eccentricity of the orbit.

  - Plot Earth and the orbit of the mission

to a correct scale on your graphing device and observe the eccentricity.

- Write an evaluation of the reporter's comment on the basis of your observations.

✦ Modeling the Rendezvous with *Mir*

When we search the World Wide Web for NASA's orbital data from the October 1995 docking between the Space Shuttle *Atlantis* and the Russian space station *Mir*, we find the following Keplerian data:

	Orbital Element	
	Semimajor Axis a	Eccentricity e
Atlantis	6 718 397.21 m	0.0003878
Mir	6 774 825.37 m	0.0012407

Convert the measure of the semimajor axes to miles. With the polar-coordinate equation for orbits, and using 3 960 miles for the radius of Earth, plot the following on your graphing device:

- Earth

- The orbit of *Atlantis*

- The orbit of *Mir*

Find a small window that allows you to investigate the distance between *Atlantis* and *Mir*. Using your set of equations, make some calculations of the distance separating *Atlantis* and *Mir*. Compare your results with news reports on such important items as altitude for each spacecraft and time for a complete orbit.

✦ Modeling the Orbit of the Moon

Orbital elements for the Moon are semimajor axis of orbit = 244 900 miles and eccentricity of orbit = 0.0549. Use 4 000 miles for the radius of Earth and try to superimpose the Moon's orbit on the outline of Earth. As you can guess, the scale of your window is critical here. You may want to start with a scale of 1 = 1 000 miles.

Trace your orbit of the Moon to determine perigee and apogee. Compare your perigee and apogee readings with values you find in an astronomy table.

✦ Exploring the Solar System

Use the polar equation of an ellipse and your graphing device to plot the orbits of the planets around the Sun. Use the information from this table or from any similar chart of solar system data:

Planet	Semimajor Axis (a) in AU*	Eccentricity (e)
Mercury	0.3871	0.2056
Venus	0.7233	0.0068
Earth	1.000*	0.0167
Mars	1.524	0.0934
Jupiter	5.203	0.0484
Saturn	9.539	0.0543
Uranus	19.18	0.046
Neptune	30.06	0.0082
Pluto	39.44	0.2481

* An astronomical unit (AU) is equal to the distance between Earth and the Sun, about 93 000 000 miles.

Choosing a scale for your graphing window(s) is very important. Begin with the inner planets and see how far you can go in plotting orbits until the inner orbits "vanish." What is the minimum number of windows needed to get a nice display of the planets' orbits?

Use a special window to study the orbits of Neptune and Pluto only. Part of your viewing window should suggest an astronomical event that occurred on 21 January 1979, will next occur on 14 March 1999, and then will not happen again until September 2226. The behavior that better identifies the event may be hidden. Make a guess about what the event is, then zoom in to decide if the event is indeed possible. You may also want to investigate perihelion and aphelion for both planets. Note that perihelion and aphelion are the points in the planet's orbit nearest and farthest from the Sun (from the Greek *helios*); they are analagous to perigee and apogee in an orbit around Earth.

✦ For Experts Only!

We know that the models we have looked at greatly simplify the actual orbit. Depending on the orientation of Earth, all orbits plotted so far appear to be going over the poles. Since we launch from the Kennedy Space Center in Florida, we know that our satellite orbits are inclined at an angle.

- Alter your parametric or polar equation(s) to graph an orbit inclined at an angle of 28 degrees.

- The ground track for such an orbit is sinusoidal. Suppose that the *x*-axis of this sine curve is a horizontal line through Cape Canaveral, Florida, and that the greatest displacement of the ground track from this line is 1000 miles. If the spacecraft makes a complete orbit every ninety minutes, write an equation to model the ground track and plot it on your graphing utility.

- Superimpose your sine wave on a Mercator projection map of the world to produce a plot similar to the one that follows.

- Plot sine waves on a Mercator projection map of the world to model the ground tracks of orbits over a full twenty-four-hour day or for a complete NASA mission.

- Compare your picture with the big-screen image we often see in pictures from Mission Control in Houston.

Mission Control Center

ADVANCED COMMUNICATION SYSTEMS

Our improved ability to receive television signals in our homes is one visible example of how NASA's research in advanced communication systems affects us daily. It was only a short time ago that the television signals we received originated from a limited number of local and network television stations. Those stations used omnidirectional broadcast systems, which were limited in radiating their broadcast signals to the geographic horizon. These signals decayed in strength in relation to the square of the distance from the station to the receiver. Hills, valleys, and buildings also interfered with those straight-line signals.

Home television reception of many channels and an improved signal are products of communications technology developed and tested in orbit by NASA in the 1960s and 1970s. This effort led to the development, manufacture, and operation of commercial communication satellites. Satellite communication of television signals has allowed cable television and satellite transmission to develop. Cable companies invested in powerful satellite-dish receivers and miles of cable to individual homes. These technological advances allowed the reception of many channels and improved the quality of the transmission. Some people who live in remote areas have home satellite dishes and receive satellite transmission directly into their homes. More recently, the concept of direct television has become popular even where cable and broadcast television are available. Direct television gives access to 100 or more television channels, including special "packages" of programming, such as sports.

The success of our television industry is one example of how NASA technology has affected the communications industry. Today, the United States leads the world in advanced communications systems, which has had a resultant positive impact on our economy. To remain competitive, NASA and its industry partners continue to explore new communications technologies. The purpose of this effort is to allow our communications industries to meet the needs of the world.

Another example of the joint effort of NASA and industry in the field of communications systems is the *Advanced Communications Technology Satellite (ACTS)*. This large and highly innovative communications satellite was launched in September 1993. During its time in orbit, more than eighty organizations have been undertaking advanced communications in field trials designed to increase communications performance while reducing operational costs. The results of these trials indicate that potential exists to make practicable such services as remote medical-imaging diagnostics, global personal communications, real-time television for airliners, the direct transmission of image data to battlefield commanders, the interconnection of distantly located supercomputers, and high-speed off-ramps for the National Information Infrastructure. NASA continues to provide the technology that fuels the communications industry, an important segment of our economy.

COMMUNICATING THROUGH SPACE

We have all, at one time or another, watched in awe as pictures and messages were transmitted from space, whether it was Neil Armstrong's "one small step" on the surface of the Moon, a satellite's close-up view of a distant planet, or the Hubble Telescope's observation of galaxies billions of light-years away. We have seen men and women as they walked in space or performed experiments aboard the Space Shuttle, and we have listened to live communications between Mission Control and the orbiting astronauts. But have we wondered deeply about how such messages, be they pictures or sounds or data from instrument readings, come to us across the vast distances of space?

NASA does not, of course, beam back tiny canisters of film to be developed or cassettes of videotape to be rewound and played. Rather, the transmission of information from space is accomplished through the technology of telemetry, whereby data from cameras and sensors are converted into radio pulses that are transmitted to receivers on Earth and relayed to data centers where the radio pulses are converted back into their original formats.

PURPOSES

In this unit, we explore some of the problems associated with communication through space and the mathematics that enables scientists to solve those problems. The activities in this cluster investigate several aspects of the following fundamental goals: to transmit large amounts of data over long distances in a noisy environment and to decode and interpret the messages with confidence.

GETTING STARTED

Before you begin the activities in this unit, have students examine some photographs from a newspaper using a magnifying lens. Note how the photographs are composed of a field of tiny dots in various shades from white to black. The pictures on a television screen are composed in much the same way. In the case of television, long rows of dots called picture elements, or *pixels,* are rapidly illuminated by a modulated beam of light that fills one line after another in quick succession, lighting up the individual pixels at various intensities to create the picture.

Images transmitted from space are closely related to television transmissions. When a spacecraft sends pictures from space, an onboard camera system measures the intensity of light reflected from the object and converts it into numerical data that can be relayed to Earth. To accomplish this, reflected light from the object being photographed falls on the surface of a television tube that is divided into 800 parallel lines, each containing 800 pixels—a total of 640 000 pixels for each image. Each of these 640 000 pixels is then scanned for brightness and assigned a number from 0 through 255. The 256 numbers in this range correspond to shades of gray ranging from white (0) to black (255).

Once values are assigned to all the pixels, they either are transmitted to a receiver on Earth or are stored on magnetic tape for transmission at a later time. Delayed transmission may be necessary if, for example, the spacecraft is about to pass behind a planet where signals would be blocked. Radio signals to Earth are received by a system of large dish antennas called the Deep Space Network (DSN), which is made up of three stations around the globe at locations approximately 120 degrees apart: one at Goldstone, California; a second near Madrid, Spain; and the third near Canberra, Australia. From these locations, the DSN is capable of providing twenty-four-hour coverage, since as antennas at one location lose contact because of Earth's rotation, another station is in position to take up the reception.

Curriculum Connections:

Discrete Mathematics

Statistics

Algebra

Mathematical Structure

Teaching Tip: *Because much of the discrete mathematics in this unit will be unfamiliar to many high school students, the student pages include background information to introduce the topics. You can either incorporate that information into your classroom presentation or reproduce the pages for use by the students.*

Technology Tip: *The number 255 is equal to $2^8 - 1$, the largest number that can be represented by an 8-digit binary numeral. Such 8-digit, or 8-bit, units constitute a byte, the most common counting unit in computer systems.*

Photograph of Saturn transmitted from Voyager 1

An artist's concept showing Pioneer 11 flying past Saturn.

Data received by the DSN antennas are relayed to the Jet Propulsion Laboratory in Pasadena, California, which manages the DSN. There, computers re-create the images by reading the data, bit by bit, and calculating the values for each pixel; those values are then converted back into small squares of light that recompose the original image.

MATHEMATICAL CONSIDERATIONS: AN OVERVIEW

The first problem encountered in sending pictures back to Earth is quite obvious: the amount of data to be transmitted is enormous. For one picture, the 640 000 pixels require 640 000 bytes, or 5 120 000 bits, of information. Each bit is a binary digit, either 0 or 1, which is analogous to an electrical switch being either off or on. Even when data are transmitted at the rate of 100 000 bits per second, it takes nearly one minute to send a single image.

Other factors must be considered as well. Distance, for example, affects the quality of transmissions because data radioed from farther away are more prone to errors and interruptions. One way to counteract this problem is to slow the rate of data transmission, but that means a corresponding increase in the time needed to send each image. Another technique used by NASA is to compress the data so that fewer bits of information are required for each picture. We deal with data compression in the first set of activities that follow.

Another consideration concerns errors that enter into the transmission when the radio signals are sent through the noisy environment of space in which extraneous or erroneous information can be introduced. How can a receiver on Earth detect and correct for such errors? That question is addressed in the second set of activities.

Keep in mind also that photographs taken from spacecraft are often shot while the vehicle is traveling tens of thousands of miles per hour. To keep the cameras focused on their targets to get unblurred images requires stabilizing gyroscopes to rotate the entire spacecraft so that the cameras can track their objects. We do not address the question of tracking because our goal in this cluster is to focus on data transmission.

Note that all the activities in this unit involve the transmission of black-and-white images. When color images are sent, the process becomes more complex and the data considerations escalate. Color images require three black-and-white frames in succession, each taken by the onboard camera through a different filter, usually blue, green, and orange. The green filter, for example, makes the green values in the image appear brighter than the other colors. When interpreted by computers on Earth, the three images receive their appropriate color enhancements; the three are blended to form a single colored picture.

PART 1: DATA COMPRESSION

The data-compression section opens by presenting information about the use of data compression to solve problems on the recent *Galileo* mission. It also offers some insight into the magnitude of the problem of transmitting massive amounts of data in a reasonable time.

"Computers and Codes" leads students to the activity "Letters! We Get Lots and Lots of Letters!" in which they construct a frequency table for the occurrence of letters of the alphabet in English text. The results of this activity will be used in future activities related to data compression. To introduce the "Letters" activity, discuss with your students the questions of which letters appear with the greatest or least frequency in the English language. Have the students complete the individual letter-frequency chart. After they have finished counting the characters in their samples, combine the results from all pairs of students to complete the class letter-frequency chart. The results should be similar to table 10 (taken

Solutions:
Data Transmission in the News—*Galileo*
1. 134 000 bits per second
2. 16 bits per second
3. 160 bits per second
4. ~0.0012, or 0.12 percent
5. 5 120 000 bits
6. ~38.2 seconds
7. 1 919 448 seconds = ~531 hours = ~22 days
8. 320 000 seconds = ~89 hours = ~3.7 days
9. 1.6×10^{10} seconds = ~4 450 000 hours = ~185 000 days = ~507 years
10. ~8.9 hours
11. 35 555 hours = ~4 years

from "Codes and Counting" in the NCTM's *Student Math Notes*). Students should save the final letter-frequency table to use in future activities.

Table 10
Letter Frequency

Letter	Frequency (percent)	Letter	Frequency (percent)	Letter	Frequency (percent)
A	8.2	J	0.1	S	6.0
B	1.4	K	0.4	T	10.5
C	2.8	L	3.4	U	2.5
D	3.8	M	2.5	V	0.9
E	13.0	N	7.0	W	1.5
F	3.0	O	8.0	X	0.2
G	2.0	P	2.0	Y	2.0
H	5.3	Q	0.1	Z	0.07
I	6.5	R	6.8		

Mathematical Connections:
Interested students may enjoy investigating the subject of cryptography and, in particular, how letter frequencies can be used to help decode encrypted messages.

Prefix Codes

In "Prefix Codes," students are given background information about encoding data in binary format, and they are introduced to the important concept of a *prefix code* in which no code word can be confused with another. A set of code words has the *prefix property* if no code word is a prefix of any other code word.

Solutions: ✔ Your Understanding

1. { 0, 10, 11} has the prefix property.

{ 0, 100, 101, 11, 1011} does not have the prefix property because 101 is a prefix of 1011.

{ 000, 001, 10, 111, 1101} has the prefix property.

{ 00, 11, 010, 100, 011} has the prefix property.

{ 00, 10, 11, 1101, 0011} does not have the prefix property because 00 is a prefix of 0011 and 11 is a prefix of 1101.

2. Various answers are possible. One possibility is
$$+ = 00, - = 010, \times = 011, \div = 10, \angle = 110, \text{ and } \perp = 111.$$

Binary Trees

The graph theory presented in this section is limited to the development of binary trees. If you have time, you may want to present general information about graphs. Students seem to enjoy problems involving Euler and Hamiltonian circuits and vertex-coloring problems.

Finite graphs…, together with their associated matrix representations, offer an important addition to the student's repertoire of representation schemes.

(NCTM 1989, pp. 176–77)

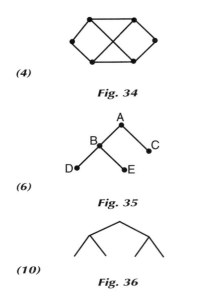

(4)

Fig. 34

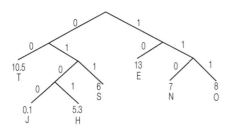

(6)

Fig. 35

(10)

Fig. 36

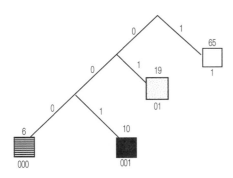

Fig. 37

Teaching Tip: Encourage students to work cooperatively in completing lengthy counting tasks.

Important concepts introduced in this section include *vertices* or *nodes* of a graph, *edges* of a graph, *degree* of a vertex, *connected* graphs, *directed* graphs or *digraphs*, *paths*, and *circuits*.

Solutions: ✔ Your Understanding

3. Degrees of A = 3, B = 3, C = 3, D = 3, E = 4
4. Various answers are possible. An example is shown in figure 34.
5. Examples: ABEDCA, ABDECA, ABDCEA
6. Various answers are possible. An example is shown in figure 35.
7. C, D, E, F, G, H
8. E, F
9. A, C, E, G, H
10. Various answers are possible. A sample answer is shown in figure 36.

Huffman's Optimal Binary Trees

The Huffman codes were among the first data-compression techniques. Data-compression technology has improved rapidly within the last twenty years, and many more techniques are now used. However, the Huffman optimal binary trees provide an elegant introduction to data compression.

Solutions: ✔ Your Understanding

11. Various answers are possible. Example: JOHNSTONE = 01001110101110011001111111010. See figure 37.

12. Words:
NOTE = 1101110010
TON = 00111110
HOST = 010111101100
SON = 011111110
NOSE = 11011101110

Pictures from Space

In the activity "Pictures from Space," students are asked to develop a Huffman code for a pseudoimage. This activity can be extended to a real NASA image, such as the picture of Saturn in the introduction to the student pages, on which students could superimpose a transparent grid and use a gray scale to code the picture.

The frequency of occurrence of the four levels of gray in "Planet with Moons" is given in table 11.

Table 11
Frequency of Gray Levels

Gray level	Number of pixels	Percent of pixels
⬜	166	65
░	49	19
☰	16	6
⬛	25	10

Fig. 38. A tree to generate code words

The tree in figure 38 generates the code words. Table 12 transforms the picture into a binary map.

Mission Mathematics: Grades 9–12

Table 12
Transformation of Picture into Binary Map

1	1	1	1	1	1	1	1	1	1	1	1	1	1	1	1
1	1	1	1	1	001	001	001	001	1	1	000	000	1	1	1
1	1	1	1	001	01	01	01	01	001	000	01	000	1	1	1
1	1	1	001	01	01	01	01	01	01	01	000	1	1	1	1
1	1	001	01	01	01	01	01	01	01	000	001	1	1	1	1
1	1	001	01	01	01	01	01	01	000	01	001	1	1	1	1
1	1	001	01	01	01	01	01	000	01	01	001	1	1	1	1
1	1	001	01	01	01	01	000	01	01	01	001	1	1	1	1
1	1	1	001	01	01	000	01	01	01	001	1	1	1	1	1
1	1	1	000	001	000	01	01	01	001	1	1	1	1	1	1
1	1	000	01	000	001	001	001	001	1	1	1	1	1	1	1
1	1	000	000	1	1	1	1	1	1	1	1	1	1	1	1
1	1	1	1	1	1	1	1	1	1	1	1	001	1	1	1
1	1	1	1	1	1	1	1	1	1	1	1	1	1	1	1
1	1	1	1	1	1	001	1	1	1	1	1	1	1	1	1
1	1	1	1	1	1	1	1	1	1	1	1	1	1	1	1

Solutions: Pictures from Space

1. $256(2) = 512$

2. $166(1) + 49(2) + 16(3) + 25(3) = 387$

3. 24.4 percent

4. If all the gray levels occurred with about the same frequencies; if the ratio of the amount of data needed to send the Huffman tree to the total amount of data is close to 1.

PART 2: ERROR DETECTION AND CORRECTION

Although not part of the traditional high school mathematics curriculum, the discrete mathematics in this section is rich with life applications and connections among number theory, geometry, abstract algebra, and matrix theory. The mathematics presented here can serve as a springboard for further study by interested students and teachers. It is mathematics that has been developed in response to the technological explosion of the twentieth century. It is mathematics that is continuing to be developed today.

The activity "Gossip" introduces this section and illustrates how errors enter into the transmission of information. Divide the class into teams of approximately eight members and have the team members form a line. A seven-digit sequence of numbers is whispered to the first member of each team, who then whispers the sequence to the next team member, who, in turn, passes the message along. Important: The message cannot be repeated to any receiver. When the message has reached the end of the line, compare the received message with the original sequence of numbers. Experiment with shorter and longer sequences of digits to determine the maximum length for a sequence to be sent free of errors and to determine the length at which very few digits are transmitted correctly.

[I]t is crucial that all students have experiences with the concepts and methods of discrete mathematics.
(NCTM 1989, p. 176)

Teaching Tip: *Most of the activities in this section are mathematically accessible to all high school students. The exception is the development of the Hamming codes, which assumes that students have experience with matrix multiplication and matrix equations. Students may need some introduction to the binary number system. They should understand the place-value system and be able to count using binary numeration.*

The concept of *redundancy*, or repetition within a communication, is also important when we attempt to detect and correct errors in messages. As an introduction, sudents can work in teams to see how many of the "Wheel of Fortune" statements they can complete. After they finish the activity, lead a class discussion about redundancy. Is there redundancy in mathematical communication? What about redundancy in visual communication? How much of a structure do we need to see before we understand what the structure is? You might want to refer to such familiar situations as crossword puzzles or the game of "hangman," in which the solver can often guess the word from a partial set of its letters, or the game "concentration," in which the solver must identify a hidden picture as parts of it are revealed bit by bit.

Solutions:

1. A cat has nine lives.
2. A bird in the hand is worth two in the bush.
3. It's raining cats and dogs!
4. You can't divide by zero.
5. A miss is as good as a mile.
6. Been there! Done that!
7. Mathematics is not a spectator sport.
8. Space exploration opens new horizons.

Hamming Distance, Binary Codes, and Parity-Check Digits

The goal of detecting and correcting errors is introduced through the problem of transmitting information about the position of a switch. Students are asked to think about how they could add redundancy to a message through the repetition of digits. This discussion leads to the concept of the *Hamming distance,* a measure of how closely one code word replicates another. Hamming distance allows us to define completely the error-correcting capability of binary linear codes.

Help students complete the chart that shows Hamming distances for the triplication code with six bits. You might want to have the students work in teams, with each team responsible for completing part of the chart. You should then carefully go through the discussion in the student pages of binary addition (exclusive or), binary linear codes, and the properties of binary linear codes. You may recognize that a binary linear code forms a group under the operation of addition. It is interesting that in these codes, each element is its own additive inverse.

Once students understand the concepts of *binary linear code* and the *weight* of a code, you can introduce the idea of using *parity* and *parity-check digits* to add redundancy to a code. Complete the development of the five-bit code using parity-check bits as outlined in the student pages.

Teaching Tip: *Define these concepts for students:*

- *The* Hamming distance *between two binary code words is the number of positions in which the digits are different.*
- *A binary linear code is a set of binary code words with the property that the sum of any code words is another code word. The minimum number of 1's is any word of the code, except the word containing all 0's, is called the* weight *of the code.*
- *A binary string has* even parity *if the sum of its bits is even and* odd parity *if the sum of its bits is odd.*

Solutions:

Hamming distance from code words:

Number of messages at distance	From code word 000000	From code word 010101	From code word 101010	From code word 111111
1	6	6	6	6
2	15	15	15	15
3	18	18	18	18
4	15	15	15	15
5	6	6	6	6

Solutions: ✔ Your Understanding

1. The binary linear codes satisfy all of the properties under the operation of addition. The identity is 000000, and each code word is its own inverse. A binary linear code forms a group under addition.

2.

+	00001	01010	10100	11111
00001	00000	01011	10101	11110
01010	01011	00000	11110	10101
10100	10101	11110	00000	01011
11111	11110	10101	01011	00000

This is not a binary linear code; it is not closed.

+	0000	0110	1011	1101
0000	0000	0110	1011	1101
0110	0110	0000	1101	1011
1011	1011	1101	0000	0110
1101	1101	1011	0110	0000

This is a binary linear code.

+	0000	0010	0111	0001	1000	1010	1101	1111
0000	0000	0010	0111	0001	1000	1010	1101	1111
0010	0010	0000	0101	0011	1010	1000	1111	1101
0111	0111	0101	0000	0110	1111	1101	1010	1000
0001	0001	0011	0110	0000	1001	1011	1100	1110
1000	1000	1010	1111	1001	0000	0010	0101	0111
1010	1010	1000	1101	1011	0010	0000	0111	0101
1101	1101	1111	1010	1100	0101	0111	0000	0010
1111	1111	1101	1000	1110	0111	0101	0010	0000

This is not a binary linear code.

3. The other possible messages are shown in the left column of the chart below, together with their distances from each code word.

	Distance from			
Message	00000	01011	10101	11110
00110	2	3	3	2
00111	3	2	2	3
01100	2	3	3	2
01101	3	2	2	3
10010	2	3	3	2
10011	3	2	2	3
11000	2	3	3	2
11001	3	2	2	3

4. Various solutions are possible. Two are given below. For the first code, let $p_1 = m_1 + m_2$, $p_2 = m_1 + m_3$, $p_3 = m_2 + m_3$. For the second code, let $p_1 = m_1 + m_2$, $p_2 = m_2 + m_3$, $p_3 = m_1 + m_2 + m_3$. The resulting codes follow.

Message	Code Word	Weight		Message	Code Word	Weight
000	000000	0		000	000000	0
001	001011	3		001	001011	3
010	010101	3		010	010111	4
011	011110	4		011	011100	3
100	100110	3		100	100101	3
101	101101	3		101	101110	4
110	110011	4		110	110010	3
111	111000	3		111	111001	4

Students come to understand the idea of [mathematical] structure through observation of the common properties in simple systems that seem on the surface to be quite dissimilar.

(NCTM 1989, p. 185)

Hamming Codes

The unit concludes with the development of *Hamming codes,* which can detect and correct one error and detect, but not correct, two errors. This section involves an application of matrices and is appropriate for students who are

Teaching Tip: *Using calculators with matrix operations or a computer spreadsheet can enhance the development of the Hamming codes.*

familiar with matrix multiplication. For students who are interested in modern algebra, the Hamming codes afford an opportunity to study Abelian groups. The decoding process involves the coset decomposition of the group.

The fundamental concept for students to develop here is that by using m parity-check digits, they can encode n message digits, where $n = 2^m - 1 - m$. The codes developed for such values of (m, n) are known as *perfect codes,* since every possible received message is at distance 1 from exactly one code word; thus all one-bit errors can be detected and corrected. The student section develops the perfect code for the case of three parity-check digits ($m = 3$) used to encode four-bit message words ($n = 4$). It also shows how the derived parity-check matrix can be used to decode messages and how good, but not perfect, single-error-correcting codes can be developed for other values of n.

Solutions: ✔ Your Understanding

5.

Message	Code Words	Message	Code Words
0000	0000000	1000	1110000
0001	1101001	1001	0011001
0010	0101010	1010	1011010
0011	1000011	1011	0110011
0100	1001100	1100	0111100
0101	0100101	1101	1010101
0110	1100110	1110	0010110
0111	0001111	1111	1111111

6.
$$\begin{bmatrix} 0001111 \\ 0110011 \\ 1010101 \end{bmatrix} \begin{bmatrix} 1 \\ 1 \\ 0 \\ 1 \\ 0 \\ 1 \\ 1 \end{bmatrix} = \begin{bmatrix} 1 \\ 1 \\ 0 \end{bmatrix}$$

6. There is an error because the syndrome is not equal to 0. Since the syndrome is equal to 6, the error is in the sixth bit. That bit is changed and the correct message is 1101001. See matrix 6 at left.

7. $Hr = \begin{bmatrix} 0 \\ 0 \\ 0 \end{bmatrix}$. The original message is correct.

8. $Hr = \begin{bmatrix} 0 \\ 0 \\ 1 \end{bmatrix}$. The first bit is incorrect. The corrected message is 1100110.

9. $Hr = \begin{bmatrix} 1 \\ 1 \\ 1 \end{bmatrix}$. The seventh bit is incorrect. The corrected message is 1111111.

10. $HU = \begin{bmatrix} 000000011111111 \\ 000111100001111 \\ 011001100110011 \\ 101010101010101 \end{bmatrix} \begin{bmatrix} p_1 \\ p_2 \\ w_1 \\ p_3 \\ w_2 \\ w_3 \\ w_4 \\ p_4 \\ w_5 \\ w_6 \\ w_7 \\ w_8 \\ w_9 \\ w_{10} \\ w_{11} \end{bmatrix}$

With 11 message bits, there will be 2^{11} messages. The parity-check equations follow:

$$p_1 = w_1 + w_2 + w_4 + w_5 + w_7 + w_9 + w_{11}$$
$$p_2 = w_1 + w_3 + w_4 + w_6 + w_7 + w_{10} + w_{11}$$
$$p_3 = w_2 + w_3 + w_4 + w_8 + w_9 + w_{10} + w_{11}$$
$$p_4 = w_5 + w_6 + w_7 + w_8 + w_9 + w_{10} + w_{11}$$

11. For three message bits we need three parity-check bits, and we use the first six columns of H_3. See matrix 11 at the right.

Message	Code Word
000	000000
001	010101
010	100110
011	110011
100	111000
101	101101
110	011110
111	001011

12.

Message	Code Word	Message	Code Word	Message	Code Word
00000	000000000	01011	110010111	10110	011001100
00001	100000011	01100	110011000	10111	111001111
00010	110100100	01101	010011011	11000	011110000
00011	010100111	01110	000111100	11001	111110011
00100	010101000	01111	100111111	11010	101010100
00101	110101011	10000	111000000	11011	001010111
00110	100001100	10001	011000011	11100	001011000
00111	000001111	10010	001100100	11101	101011011
01000	100110000	10011	101100111	11110	111111100
01001	000110011	10100	101101000	11111	011111111
01010	010010100	10101	001101011		

See matrix 12 at the right.

11. $$HU = \begin{bmatrix} 000111 \\ 011001 \\ 101010 \end{bmatrix} \begin{bmatrix} p_1 \\ p_2 \\ w_1 \\ p_3 \\ w_2 \\ w_3 \end{bmatrix}$$

where
$$\begin{aligned} p_1 &= w_1 + w_2 \\ p_2 &= w_1 + w_3 \\ p_3 &= w_2 + w_3 \end{aligned}$$

12. $$HU = \begin{bmatrix} 000000011 \\ 000111100 \\ 011001100 \\ 101010101 \end{bmatrix} \begin{bmatrix} p_1 \\ p_2 \\ w_1 \\ p_3 \\ w_2 \\ w_3 \\ w_4 \\ p_4 \\ w_5 \end{bmatrix}$$

where
$$\begin{aligned} p_1 &= w_1 + w_2 + w_4 + w_5 \\ p_2 &= w_1 + w_3 + w_4 \\ p_3 &= w_2 + w_3 + w_4 \\ p_4 &= w_5 \end{aligned}$$

0	1	2
0000	0001	0010
3	4	5
0011	0100	0101
6	7	8
0110	0111	1000

Fig. 39. Binary representation

APPLICATIONS

Long-Distance Tic-Tac-Toe

This open-ended problem has no single correct solution. This activity should be done after the unit on data compression, if possible. If students have not done the unit on data compression, you may need to help them consider the efficiency of their coding schemes. Some possible solutions follow.

Solution 1

Let the nine cells of the tic-tac-toe board be represented by the digits 0–8, beginning with 0 in the upper-left corner and 8 in the lower-right corner. Then convert these digits to their binary representation as shown in figure 39. Each cell of the board can be in one of three states: blank, X, or O. A two-digit binary code can be used to represent these three states:

$$\text{blank} = 00 \qquad X = 01 \qquad O = 10$$

In this long-distance game, a move would consist of sending six binary digits of information about each of the nine cells for a total of 54 bits. For example, the status of the board in figure 40 would be sent as 000010 000100 001000 001100 010001 010100 011000 011100 100000.

For error correction, a 3-bit parity-check code could be used, which would increase to 108 the number of bits to be sent for one move.

Solution 2

Let each cell in the tic-tac-toe board be represented by an ordered pair (r, c) where r = row and c = column of the cell. Converting to binary representation results in the board in figure 41. As in solution 1, the state of each cell will be represented as follows:

$$\text{blank} = 00 \qquad X = 01 \qquad O = 10$$

A move in this game would consist of sending 6 bits of information for each

Fig. 40. Tic-tac-toe board

(1, 1)	(1, 2)	(1, 3)
(01, 01)	**(01, 10)**	**(01, 11)**
(2, 1)	(2, 2)	(2, 3)
(10, 01)	**(10, 10)**	**(10, 11)**
(3, 1)	(3, 2)	(3, 3)
(11, 01)	**(11, 10)**	**(11, 11)**

Fig. 41. Binary representation of a tic-tac-toe board

cell, 4 bits for the (r, c) ordered pair, and 2 bits for the status. Using three parity-check bits would again increase the number of bits for each move to 108.

Solution 3

This solution recognizes that it is not necessary to send the status of the entire tic-tac-toe board to indicate the move that a player makes. If we assume either that messages are correctly received or that errors are detected and corrected, the only information that needs to be sent to indicate a move is the location of the cell where the player is going to mark either X or O. The symbol does not need to be sent because presumably each player will know who is X or O. The representation of the board used in the previous solutions will work here. Even if 3 bits are added for error correction, a move here would consist of sending only 7 bits.

Speeding Your Mail With ZIP + 4

This activity is one example of the use of codes and check digits in everyday life. The ubiquitous bar codes offer a rich area for a further study of codes through student research and products. Other examples of codes used in everyday life that could be topics for student research are the ISBN code used internationally for books; the UPC code used by merchandisers to code products for sale; the codes used by banks, airlines, automobile manufacturers, and parcel-delivery services; and the Soundex code used for genealogical research.

The bar codes and the corresponding binary representation of each digit in a ZIP code are shown in figure 42.

Decimal	Bar	Binary
1	ııı╻╻	00011
2	ıı╻ı╻	00101
3	ıı╻╻ı	00110
4	ı╻ıı╻	01001
5	ı╻ı╻ı	01010
6	ı╻╻ıı	01100
7	╻ııı╻	10001
8	╻ıı╻ı	10010
9	╻ı╻ıı	10100
0	╻╻ııı	11000

Fig. 42. Bar codes and binary representations

Solutions:

e	90210		g	39048
i	53981		c	29857
h	69794		f	45046
a	12882		d	03823
b	78964			

1. (a) 74006-8956   (f) 94035-1000
   (b) 49855-5394   (g) 32816-1250
   (c) 55437-1916   (h) 22091-1593
   (d) 68137-0662   (i) 61790-4520
   (e) 53228-1044

2. (a) 47812-9673   (b) 60610-4125

3. 35812-0001   ╻ıı╻╻ıı╻ı╻ı╻ı╻ıı╻ıııı╻╻ıı╻ı╻╻╻╻ıııı╻ıı╻╻ıı╻╻ı╻╻ııııı╻╻╻╻╻ıııı╻╻ıı╻

4. (a) The ZIP-code bar code can detect and correct any single error in a block of five bars. Two errors in a block of five bars yield two possible cases:

   (i) The two errors result in a block that is not a legitimate code word. In this case, the errors can be detected and corrected as in the case of a single error in a block.

   (ii) The two errors result in a block that is a legitimate code word. In this case, the check digit will detect the error because the sum of the digits will not be 10. However, this error cannot be corrected because it is not possible to determine which digit is in error.

   (b) If two errors occur in different blocks of the code, the errors will be detected because there is a single error in each block. These errors cannot be corrected.

   (c) A transposition error will not be detected because the check digit will give the same sum in either case.

COMMUNICATING THROUGH SPACE

This "picture" of the planet Saturn was assembled from images obtained from the *Voyager 2* spacecraft in 1981. The image is not really a photograph in the sense that we think of photographs as images recorded on film. Instead, the image is composed of a pattern of dots assigned various shades of gray, from white to black, which measure the brightness of the light reflected from the planet. The pattern of dots is similar to the one shown below, except that instead of an 8-by-9 grid, the grids used by NASA have 800 rows and 800 columns for a total of 640 000 dots, or pixels.

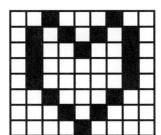

With this binary system,
white = 00000000,
gray1 = 00000001,
gray2 = 00000010,
gray254 = 11111110,
black = 11111111.

Each pixel is assigned one of 256 levels of gray. The number 256 was chosen because $256 = 2^8$, which means that each of the 256 gray levels can be encoded with 8 binary digits, or *bits*. Thus, for each image, a total of 8 • 640 000, or 5 120 000, bits, each containing either a 0 or a 1, needs to be sent. In addition, the amount of data to be sent is increased by the need to build in additional information, or *redundancy,* for error detection and correction. Finding methods to reduce the amount of data without losing information is one problem that mathematical thinking has helped to solve.

The transmission of information across the vast distances of space is subject also to various errors caused by electromagnetic interference or equipment malfunction. Thus, a second major problem that mathematics has helped solve is the challenge of detecting and correcting errors in the messages received.

These two aspects of communication, data compression and error detection and correction, represent significant applications of mathematics not only in space communications but also in numerous everyday applications. This unit introduces the fundamental concepts of that mathematics.

PART 1: DATA COMPRESSION

In 1989, NASA launched the spacecraft *Galileo* on a mission to study the planet Jupiter. Plans called for the craft to descend into orbit around Jupiter in December 1995 and to transmit information about the Jovian atmosphere as well as thousands of pictures of the giant planet. However, in 1991 the main data-transmitting antenna refused to unfurl, forcing NASA to depend on a backup antenna. Then in October 1995, a data recorder on

board the spacecraft failed, further complicating and slowing the process of data transmission. As the following excerpt from *Newsweek* magazine shows, data-compression technology and NASA engineers came to the rescue, preventing the failure of *Galileo*'s mission.

The first spacecraft to circle a giant planet for an extended time, *Galileo* will probe Jupiter's weather, photograph four of its 16 moons, investigate what makes its wind alternate direction and try to figure out what creates its colors....

All this is possible only because NASA's space jocks performed the equivalent of a long-distance brain transplant. After losing the main antenna, *Galileo* had to rely on a backup that normally transmits no more than 16 bits per second, compared with the main antenna's 134,000. At that rate, scientists would have been receiving *Galileo*'s data for years.... So, starting in March, the ground team reprogrammed *Galileo*'s computers to compress the data they sent and eliminate the boring stuff (like black pictures of empty space). Such a maneuver had never been attempted before, says the JPL's Walt Hoffman, who likens it to "upgrading your word processor while you're using it." For 26 days the computer team radioed up digital code that rewrote on-board software. It was a feat akin to sending instructions over your modem in San Jose to reprogram a computer in Tokyo—except that this computer was speeding through space at 18,000 mph. The fix upped the data rate to 160 bits per second. That should allow *Galileo* to accomplish about 70% of its goals, though it will send no more than 4,000 photos instead of the 50,000 once planned. (From "The Spacecraft That Could," *Newsweek,* 18 December 1995)

Read the excerpt from *Newsweek* and then answer the following questions:

1. What was the data transmission rate of *Galileo*'s main antenna?

2. What was the transmission rate of the backup antenna?

3. What transmission rate was NASA able to achieve after reprogramming *Galileo*'s computers?

4. What fraction of the original rate has NASA been able to achieve?

5. If each image is divided into a grid of 800-by-800 pixels, and each pixel requires 8 bits to be transmitted, how many bits are required for the transmission of one image?

6. How long would it take *Galileo* to transmit one image if the original main antenna rate was used?

7. At the original rate, how much time would have been required to transmit the 50 000 images of Jupiter that were originally planned?

8. How long would it take to transmit one image using the backup antenna if the *Galileo* software had not been altered?

9. How long would it have taken to send the 50 000 images of Jupiter if the software had not been altered?

10. How long will it take to transmit one image now that the *Galileo* software has been changed?

11. How long will it take to transmit the 4 000 images that are now planned?

Note: The assumption here is that NASA did not actually increase the transmission rate of the backup antenna because that would require a hardware change. Instead, they achieved a pseudorate of 160 bits per second (bps). That is, they compressed the data enough so that it is the equivalent of transmitting at a rate of 160 bps.

Computers and Codes

Ultimately, computers only understand binary numbers, sequences of 0's and 1's. Each pixel in a drawing or each character in a word-processor document must be translated into a binary number for the computer to understand it. The ASCII code (American Standard Code for Information Interchange) is the code that computers most frequently use for converting characters to binary numbers. In ASCII, each letter of the alphabet, each numerical digit, and each special character, like $, &, and #, is represented by a string of seven binary digits. Even though ASCII uses only seven bits, it is always represented by eight bits with a leading bit of 0.

The ASCII code is an example of a *block code* in which each symbol to be encoded is represented by the same number of binary digits. Morse code, which was invented for the telegraph and was later used in radio communication by military and amateur radio operators, is an example of a code in which the length of the code word used to represent a symbol is variable. In Morse code, frequently used letters, such as E, are represented by short codes, whereas less frequently used letters are represented by longer codes. In Morse code the average message length is shorter than it would be if a block code were used.

The method of using longer code words for less frequently used symbols and shorter code words for more frequently used symbols is one form of data compression. To explore how the frequency of letters of the alphabet affects codes, complete the activity "Letters! We Get Lots and Lots of Letters!"

Examples of ASCII code:
A = 01000001
B = 01000010
C = 01000011
a = 01100001
b = 01100010
c = 01100011
1 = 00110001
2 = 00110010
% = 00100101
$ = 00100110

Examples of Morse code:

E = •

Z = — — • •

Letters! We Get Lots and Lots of Letters!

Suppose that you picked up a newspaper or a book and counted the number of times each letter in the alphabet appeared.

- Which letter do you think would appear most frequently? _____
- Which letters would rank in the top five in frequency of occurrence? _____
- Which letter do you think would appear least frequently? _____
- Which letters would rank in the bottom five in frequency of occurrence? _____

Obtain a sample of text from your teacher and, with your partner, do the following.

1. Mark the text in groups of ten letters. Continue until you have counted 300 letters. For example:

> A giant, gase | ous planet, S | aturn has an | intriguing | atmosphere.

2. Use tally marks to count the number of times each letter occurs in your text sample and complete the individual letter-frequency chart. An easy way to do this is for one partner to read the letter and the other partner to mark the tally on the chart.

3. Combine your results with those of other pairs of students in the class and complete the class letter-frequency chart. Save this chart for future use.

4. How close to your predictions are the class results? How many of the top five letters did you predict? How many of the bottom five did you guess?

INDIVIDUAL LETTER-FREQUENCY CHART
(Based on 300 Characters of English Text)

Letter	Tally	Total	Frequency Percent	Letter	Tally	Total	Frequency Percent
A				N			
B				O			
C				P			
D				Q			
E				R			
F				S			
G				T			
H				U			
I				V			
J				W			
K				X			
L				Y			
M				Z			

CLASS LETTER-FREQUENCY CHART
(Based on _____ Characters of English Text)

Letter	Tally	Total	Frequency Percent	Letter	Tally	Total	Frequency Percent
A				N			
B				O			
C				P			
D				Q			
E				R			
F				S			
G				T			
H				U			
I				V			
J				W			
K				X			
L				Y			
M				Z			

5. Write a paragraph summarizing the results shown on the class letter-frequency chart.

Prefix Codes

Suppose that you want to encode the word *SPACE* in a binary code, such as the one below.

A = 0   C = 1   E = 01   P = 10   S = 11

The encoded word would be 11100101. Next, suppose that you have received this coded message; try to decode it. Reading from the left, 11 could signify the letter S or it could be the double letters CC; the next two bits, 10, could be the single character P or the two characters C and A. There is no way to tell how to decode in this situation.

Examine the following code for the same letters:

A = 11   C = 10   E = 01   P = 001   S = 000

Encoded, the word *SPACE* becomes 000001111001. This time, there is no question about how to decode. Only one word is possible: *SPACE*.

As the message is scanned from left to right, the procedure is as follows:	
0	Not a word
00	Not a word
000	= S
0	Not a word
00	Not a word
001	= P
.	
.	
.	
11	= A
10	= C
01	= E

What is the difference between these two codes that makes unique decoding possible in the latter example? The second code has what is known as the *prefix property*.

A set of code words has the prefix property if no code word is a prefix of any other code word.

In the first code, A = 0 is a prefix of E = 01, and C = 1 is a prefix of both P = 10 and S = 11. In the second code, A = 11 is not a prefix of any other code word, C = 10 is not a prefix of any code word, and so on.

✔ Your Understanding:

1. Which of the following sets of code words have the prefix property?

    { 0, 10, 11}
    { 0, 100, 101, 11, 1011}
    { 000, 001, 10, 111, 1101}
    { 00, 11, 010, 100, 011}
    { 00, 10, 11, 1101, 0011}

2. Create a code for the symbols +, −, ×, ÷, ∠, and ⊥ that has the prefix property.

Binary Trees

How can we produce codes for letters and symbols that compress data as much as possible without introducing ambiguity? One of the earliest techniques employed a device known as a *binary tree*, which is a special kind of mathematical structure called a *graph*. A graph is a set of points called *vertices* or *nodes* and a set of line segments called *edges*. Shown below are examples of graphs that we shall use to introduce vocabulary associated with graphs and to observe some of the properties of graphs.

In graph 1, the vertices are *A, B, C,* and *D* and the edges are *AB, AC,* and *BC.* The *degree* of a vertex is the number of edges at that vertex. In graph 1, vertices *A, B,* and *C* each have degree 2, and *D* has degree 0. Graphs 2 and 3 are called *connected* graphs because every vertex has degree greater than or equal to 1. Graph 1 is not connected because vertex *D* is isolated.

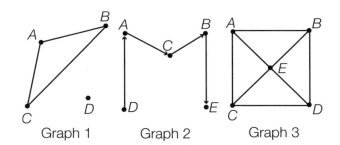

Graph 1   Graph 2   Graph 3

Mathematicians speak of *traversing* a graph by moving from one vertex to another along the edges of the graph. Such a traversal is called a *path*. In graph 3, a path from vertex A to vertex D is *ABECD*. Another path is *AED*. Paths that traverse a graph and return to the starting vertex are called *circuits*. In graph 1, the path *ACBA* is a circuit, and in graph 3, *AECA* is a circuit. Graph 2 has no circuits.

Graph 2 is called a *directed graph* or *digraph*. The arrows along the edges indicate that one must move in the direction of the arrows in traversing the graph. In a directed graph, the number of edges leading into a vertex is called its *in-degree* and the number of edges leading away from the vertex is called its *out-degree*. In graph 2, vertex D has in-degree equal to 0 and out-degree equal to 1; vertices A, B, and C have in-degree equal to 1 and out-degree equal to 1; vertex E has in-degree equal to 1 and out-degree equal to 0.

✔ Your Understanding:

3. What is the degree of each vertex in graph 3?

4. Draw an example of a connected graph with six vertices in which each vertex has a degree of at least 2.

5. In graph 3, find a circuit that passes only once through each vertex.

6. Draw an example of a directed graph with five vertices and the following properties:

- The graph is connected with no circuits.

- Vertex A has in-degree equal to 0 and out-degree equal to 1 or 2.

- Vertices B, C, D, and E have in-degree equal to 1 and out-degree equal to 0, 1, or 2.

The graph that satisfies the foregoing requirements is an example of a *binary tree*.

Binary trees are similar to real trees in that they have a *root, branches,* and *leaves.* They are also similar to the familiar family tree used in genealogy. The languages of biology and genealogy are both used in describing binary trees.

A binary tree is a directed graph that satisfies the following conditions.

- ◆ The graph is connected.
- ◆ There are no circuits in the graph.
- ◆ The number of edges is one less than the number of vertices.
- ◆ There is a single vertex, called the *root,* which has in-degree equal to 0 and out-degree equal to 1 or 2.
- ◆ All other vertices have in-degree equal to 1 and out-degree equal to 0, 1, or 2.

In the binary trees below, R is the *root node.* Note the absence of arrows showing the direction of travel in these diagrams. As in most binary trees, it is understood that the direction of travel is downward from the root to the other vertices.

In tree 1, A is known as the *left-child* of R and B is the *right-child* of R. Node G is the left-child of C, whereas C has no right-child. Node D is known as the *parent* of H and I. Node B is the *ancestor* of the nodes E, J, F, K, L, and M; these same nodes are known as *descendants* of B. The nodes G, H, I, J, K, and M, which have no children, are called *leaves.*

Examples of Binary Trees

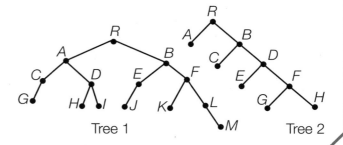

Tree 1   Tree 2

✔ Your Understanding:

7. Name the descendants of *B* in tree 2.

8. Name the children of *D* in tree 2.

9. Name the leaves of tree 2.

10. Draw a binary tree with seven nodes such that four nodes are leaves.

Huffman's Optimal Binary Trees

In the 1950s, David Huffman found a way to create binary trees that describe a compression code for data in which the expected frequencies of the symbols to be transmitted are known in advance. Suppose that the characters *E, A, C, O,* and *T* are to be transmitted and that the expected frequencies of these characters are as follows:

E: 30%   A: 25%   C: 20%   O: 15%   T: 10%

The procedure for creating a Huffman tree follows:

(i) Consider the two smallest frequencies, including frequencies of previously formed trees. In this case, the frequencies are 10 percent and 15 percent. Resolve ties arbitrarily.

(ii) Form a binary tree with the smallest frequency on the left and the next smallest frequency on the right. The sum of these two frequencies will become the root of a new tree; the sum becomes one of the frequencies under consideration.

(iii) Repeat steps i and ii with the two smallest remaining frequencies until all frequencies have been used and a single binary tree has been formed.

The steps in constructing the Huffman tree for the foregoing data follow:

✦ The frequencies are {10, 15, 20, 25, 30}.

A node is formed by adding the two smallest frequencies, 10 and 15. Now the frequencies are {20, 25, 25, 30}.

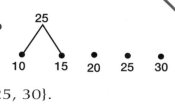

✦ The smallest frequencies are now 20, 25, and 25. We arbitrarily choose the frequency from the previously completed node and form a new node with a sum of 45. A different but equivalent tree would be formed if we chose the other 25. The remaining frequencies are now {25, 30, 45}.

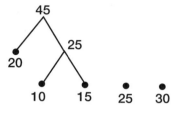

✦ A node is next formed from the two smallest frequencies, 25 and 30. The remaining frequencies are now 45 and 55. Notice that temporarily we have two trees.

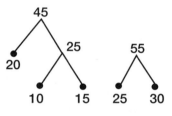

✦ The frequencies 45 and 55 are now combined to form the root of the tree with a frequency of 100.

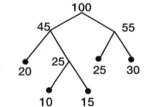

Here are two completed Huffman trees constructed using the following sets of frequencies: (*a*) {5, 10, 15, 25, 45} and (*b*) {1, 4, 9, 16, 25, 36}. Study these examples to ensure that you understand the algorithm for constructing the Huffman tree.

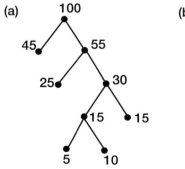

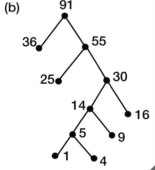

Let us return to the tree constructed with frequencies {10, 15, 20, 25, 30}. We shall use the tree to encode words. We begin by replacing each of the original frequencies with its corresponding symbol in the tree. Then we assign 0 to each left-child and 1 to each right-child for each node of the tree. By beginning at the root and following the tree to each leaf, we have a code word for each letter:

$$C = 00 \quad T = 010 \quad O = 011 \quad A = 10 \quad E = 11$$

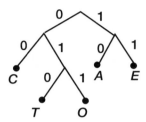

Note that E, A, and C, which occur with greater frequency, have the shortest code words, whereas T and O have longer code words. This code also has the prefix property. Huffman trees always give a prefix code, and they yield the most efficient code for the given frequencies.

◆ Suppose that we want to use the code to encode the word *CAT*. The code would be 0010010.

◆ We have been given the code 100011 to decode. We start at the root of the tree, and follow the path indicated by

the code until we reach a code word. Then we go back to the root and begin the process again. In this case, 10 leads to A, 00 leads to C, and 11 leads to E. Thus, we have decoded *ACE*.

✔ **Your Understanding:**

11. Use the letter-frequency chart from the activity "Letters! We Get Lots and Lots of Letters!" to create your own Huffman tree. Begin by writing the letters in your last name. Below each letter write the frequency of occurrence according to your letter-frequency chart; each letter in your name will occur only once in the tree even if it is repeated in your name. Construct a Huffman tree using these weights. Assign 0 to each left-child and 1 to each right-child in your tree, and encode your last name using the Huffman code you created.

12. Try to make some words from the letters in your name. Encode them using your Huffman tree. Give the tree and the coded words to a classmate to decode.

You are now ready to do the activity "Pictures from Space," a more complex example of the use of Huffman trees.

PICTURES FROM SPACE

The picture shown below, *Planet with Moons,* was created using four levels of gray, as shown. The image contains a total of 16 × 16 = 256 pixels. Count the frequency of occurrence of each level of gray and complete the frequency chart.

Planet with Moons

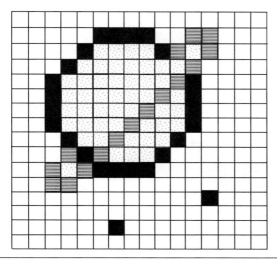

Gray Level	Number of Pixels	Percent of Pixels
⬜		
▦		
▤		
⬛		

Use your frequency chart to construct a Huffman tree for the gray levels and the weights you have calculated; use your tree to encode the image for data transmission. Begin with the first row in the grid and move across each row; move to the next row and go across that row. Continue until all sixteen rows have been encoded.

Use the 16 × 16 grid to create your own picture using the four gray levels as before. Encode your picture using a Huffman tree and give the coded image to another student to decode.

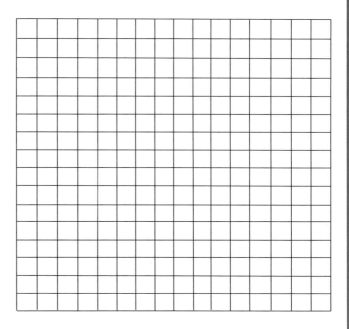

Answer the following questions about the picture *Planet with Moons* and about your own picture. Suppose that the uncompressed data were to be sent as a two-bit code where

⬜ = 00, ▦ = 01, ▤ = 10, and ⬛ = 11.

1. How many bits would be required to transmit the image in uncompressed form?

2. How many bits would be required using the Huffman code?

3. What is the percent reduction in the number of bits?

4. The Huffman code is not always the best answer for data compression. What are some situations in which the Huffman tree would not lead to a significant savings in data transmission?

PART 2: ERROR DETECTION AND CORRECTION

The transmission of information between Earth and a spacecraft is subject to various errors caused by electromagnetic interference or equipment malfunction. The situation is similar to the old game "gossip," in which a message is whispered to a participant who in turn whispers it to the next participant and so on until the last participant has received the message. Frequently, the last message has little resemblance to the starting message. At the end of the game, the original message is compared with the final one and everyone has a good laugh. In transmissions from space, scientists and engineers have found that it is virtually impossible to ensure that the received message is identical to the message that was sent. However, they have developed techniques that can detect and correct errors in the transmission of information.

Try this: "Gossip"

Have the members of your team form a line. The first member of the team writes down a sequence of seven digits and whispers the sequence to the second person, who in turn whispers the message to the third person, and so on. No repeats of the message are allowed. The last person in the line writes down the sequence she or he has received. Compare the original message with the message received by the last person. Did errors occur in transmission?

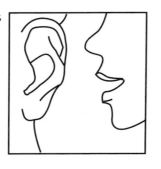

Repeat this process several times with seven-digit sequences. Then experiment with sequences of fewer digits and sequences of more digits.

What did you discover? Was some length of sequence transmitted accurately most of the time? Did some length of sequence always seem to have errors in transmission? What do you think causes the transmission errors? Is there more than one source of error? The problems you encountered with transmissions of data in the gossip activity are similar to the problems encountered by NASA in the transmission of data to and from space. In this unit, you will learn some of the ways that mathematics helps NASA detect and correct errors in the transmission of data.

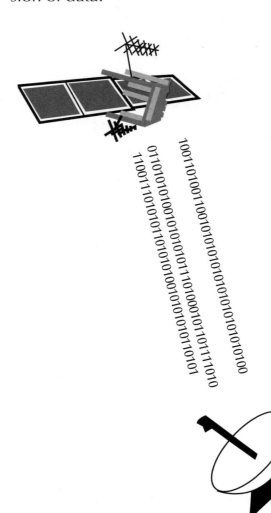

Redundancy in Human Communication

In written and oral communication, errors are detected and corrected because of built-in redundancies in language. Letters or even entire words can be omitted or be written or spoken incorrectly and the reader or listener can still understand what the message is trying to say. It is this built-in redundancy that has made the television game show *Wheel of Fortune* successful. The home viewer may be amazed that she or he can so often determine the hidden message when only a few letters have been revealed. This feat is not really that amazing; it is simply an example of redundancy in the English language.

Try this: Work with your team members to complete as many of the following phrases as you can. Most are familiar proverbs or idiomatic expressions, such as "A stitch in time saves nine."

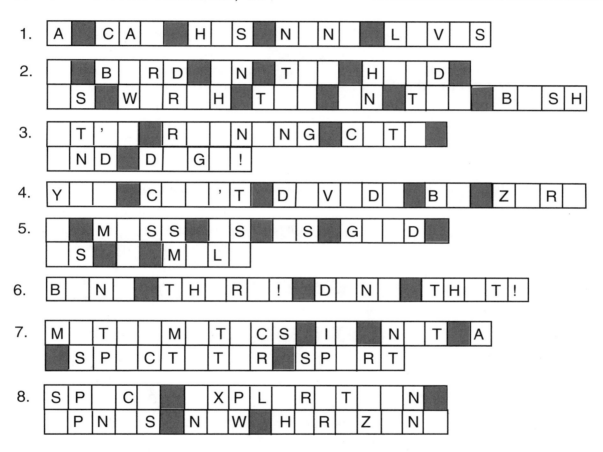

Music, another mode of communication, also has built-in redundancies that make it possible for trained musicians, and sometimes even untrained listeners, to detect errors. A really sour note is obvious to all listeners even though they may not immediately know how to fix it. It has been said that the professional musician is not one who never makes mistakes but is one who knows how to cover up mistakes so they are not noticed. The musician is doing his or her own error correction.

Mathematicians and engineers have used various methods to build redundancy into communication. A simplified diagram of the process of error correction is shown on the next page.

Experimenting with Error Detection and Correction: The Switch

Imagine that you are the controller for an unmanned Earth-orbiting satellite and that you need to know the position of a certain switch on the spacecraft. The spacecraft transmits all information in the form of strings of binary digits, that is, sequences of 0's and 1's, where 0 means switch off and 1 means switch on.

Suppose that you receive a 0 from the spacecraft, indicating that the switch is off. Is the 0 correct? How would you know? What could you do to increase the likelihood of receiving a correct message? Can you think of a way to add redundancy to the message so that you are able to detect and correct one error?

One form of redundancy is to repeat the message. That is, off = 0 would be sent as 00; on = 1 would be sent as 11. If the received message is 10 or 01, we know that an error has occurred, but we do not know which bit, or digit, is in error. The error can be detected but not corrected. Of course, if two errors have occurred and 00 is received as 11 or vice versa, we will never know about the problem. By assuming that only one error will occur, we have a code that will detect one error.

Repeating the same message three times so that off = 0 would be sent as 000 and on = 1 would be sent as 111 improves our ability to correct and detect errors. If the received message is 100, 010, or 001, we know that an error has occurred; if

000
(Original message)

↓

Encoder

↓

000001
(Encoder adds redundancy.)

↓

Transmitter

↓

000001
(Transmitter sends encoded message.)

↓

—————

(An error is made somewhere in transmission. The receiver gets an incorrect message.)

—————

↓

Receiver

↓

100001

↓

Decoder

↓

000
(Decoder uses redundancy to detect and correct the error. Original message is recovered.)

we assume that only one error occurred, we can say that the switch is off. If the received message is 011, 101, or 110, we know that an error has occurred; if we assume that only one error has occurred, we can say that the switch is on. Thus, by replicating the message three times, we have a code that will correct all one-bit errors. This ability comes at a price, however, since we have to send three times the amount of information. This may not seem like a large problem in the case of the switch, but in reality, the amount of information to be transmitted is very large. Tripling that quantity could be very costly.

A More Complex Control

Imagine that you are still the controller for the unmanned spacecraft of the previous activity. This time, however, the control has four positions, called A, B, C, and D. To transmit the position of the control, you will use the following binary code.

00 = position A
01 = position B
10 = position C
11 = position D

Suppose that you receive the message 01 from the spacecraft, indicating that the control is in position B. How do you know that the message is correct? What could you do to build in redundancy so that one-bit errors could be detected and corrected?

A logical step is to try duplicating the message. That is, 00 would be sent as 0000, 01 as 0101, 10 as 1010, and 11 as 1111. You should be able to analyze this code, however, and determine that it would not result in a one-bit error correction. For example, suppose that 10 is sent as 1010. An error occurs in the first digit so that the received message is 0010. The receiver would not know whether the sent message was 0000 or 1010, since both differ from the received message in only one position.

The next step might be to triplicate the message. Here 00 would be sent as 000000, 01 as 010101, 10 as 101010, and 11 as 111111. This code will indeed work, although an analysis is more difficult. If the received message is 001000, then it would be obvious that it should be decoded as 000000. But what if the received message is 010011? How should the message be decoded? To help in the analysis, we shall define the concept of *Hamming distance*. Hamming distance is very important, since it completely defines the error-correcting capability of binary linear codes.

Hamming Distance

The Hamming distance between two binary code words is the number of positions in which the digits are different. This number is named in honor of Richard Hamming, who first developed the concept in the late 1940s.

The first table below represents the code words 000100 and 111010, which have a Hamming distance of 5 because they differ in the first five positions. In the second table, the code words 000100 and 100100 have a Hamming distance of 1 because they differ only in the first position. The idea of Hamming distance can be used to help analyze the code obtained by triplicat-

ing the message bits 00, 01, 10, and 11 to produce the code words 000000, 010101, 101010, and 111111.

> **Try this:** Complete the table on the next page to show the set of all sixty possible six-digit binary strings other than the four code words and the Hamming distance of each string from each of the four code words 000000, 010101, 101010, and 111111. You may want to share the work on this one with one or two classmates.

Your completed table will show that each code word has six possible message words that are a distance of 1 from the code word and fifteen possible messages that are a distance of 2 from the code word. Thus, this code can detect and correct all one-bit errors. It can also detect and correct some two-bit errors. However, it cannot detect and correct all two-bit errors.

Because the goal was one-bit error correction, and tripling the code is expensive in terms of the number of digits that must be transmitted, the question is whether some code with fewer digits can give one-bit error correction. The answer is yes. There is a more efficient error-correcting code for the two-bit messages 00, 01, 10, and 11. Since four bits were insufficient to detect one-bit errors, and six bits were more than we needed, it seems logical to assume that an optimal code for one-bit error correction might have five bits. To understand how to find such a code, it is necessary to know some of the mathematics and vocabulary of error-correcting codes.

> As an example, suppose that 111101 is the received message. We can assume that a one-bit error occurred and decode the message as 111111, but it is possible that two errors occurred and that the actual message sent was 010101.

0	0	0	1	0	0
1	1	1	0	1	0
✓	✓	✓	✓	✓	

0	0	0	1	0	0
1	0	0	1	0	0
✓					

HAMMING DISTANCE FROM CODE WORDS

Message Received	Distance from 000000	Distance from 010101	Distance from 101010	Distance from 111111	Message Received	Distance from 000000	Distance from 010101	Distance from 101010	Distance from 111111
000001	1	2	4	5	111110				
000010	1	4	2	5	111101				
000100					111011				
001000					110111	5	2	4	1
010000					101111	5	4	2	1
100000					011111	5	2	4	1
000011					111100	4	3	3	2
000101					111010				
001001					110110	4	3	3	2
010001					101110				
100001	2	3	3	4	011110				
000110					111001	4	3	3	2
001010	2	5	1	4	110101				
010010					101101	4	3	3	2
100010					011101				
001100					110011	4	3	3	2
010100					101011				
100100					011011				
011000	2	3	3	4	100111				
101000					010111				
110000					001111				
000111					111000	3	4	2	3
001011					110100	3	2	4	3
010011					101100				
100011					011100				
001101					110010	3	4	2	3
100101	3	2	4	3	011010				
011001					100110				
101001					010110				
110001	3	2	4	3	001110				

SUMMARY OF HAMMING DISTANCES FROM CODE WORDS

Number of messages at distance	From code word 000000	From code word 010101	From code word 101010	From code word 111111
1	6			
2				
3				
4				
5				

Addition of Binary Code Words

The addition of binary code words is a special form of addition with no "carrying," or regrouping. In Boolean logic, this operation is called "exclusive or." The rule is $0 + 0 = 1 + 1 = 0$ and $1 + 0 = 0 + 1 = 1$.

An example of adding binary code words:

$$\begin{array}{r} 00101 \\ +11011 \\ \hline 11110 \end{array}$$

A *binary linear code* is a set of binary code words with the property that the sum of any code words is another code word. The two codes developed in "The Switch" and "A More Complex Control" are examples of binary linear codes. Addition tables for those two codes are shown at right and below.

Addition Table for Code {000, 111}

+	000	111
000	000	111
111	111	000

Addition Table for Code
{000000, 010101, 101010, 111111}

+	000000	010101	101010	111111
000000	000000	010101	101010	111111
010101	010101	000000	111111	101010
101010	101010	111111	000000	010101
111111	111111	101010	010101	000000

Algebra Connection: Recall the fundamental properties of the operation of addition for real numbers:

Closure: The sum of any two real numbers is a real number.

Commutative property: $a + b = b + a$

Associative property: $a + (b + c) = (a + b) + c$

Identity property: There exists a number 0, such that $0 + a = a + 0 = a$ for all numbers a.

Inverses property: For every number a there is a number $-a$ such that $a + (-a) = -a + a = 0$.

- Is every sum a code word?
- Is the addition commutative?
- Is the addition associative?
- Is there an identity?
- Does every code word have an inverse?

✔ Your Understanding:

1. Which of these properties do the foregoing two codes satisfy under the operation of addition?

2. Complete the addition tables for the following codes. Which of these codes are binary linear codes?

+	00001	01010	10100	11111
00001				
01010				
10100				
11111				

+	0000	0110	1011	1101
0000				
0110				
1011				
1101				

+	0000	0010	0111	0001	1000	1010	1101	1111
0000								
0010								
0111								
0001								
1000								
1010								
1101								
1111								

Which of the properties hold?

Which of the properties fail?

Binary linear codes have some properties that make it easier to design error-correcting codes. Looking again at the code {000000, 010101, 101010, 111111}, we can see that the distance between any pair of code words is at least 3. For example, 010101 is at a distance of 3 from 000000 and 111111, and it is at a distance of 6 from 101010. We also note that except for the code word 000000, the minimum number of 1's in any code word is three. This is no coincidence.

For a binary linear code, the minimum distance between code words equals the minimum number of 1's in any code word except for the word containing all 0's. This minimum number of 1's is called the *weight* of the code. The weight of a binary linear code provides a simple way to determine the error-detecting and error-correcting capability of the code:

To *detect* k errors, a binary linear code must have a weight of at least $k + 1$. To *correct* k errors, the weight of the code must be at least $2k + 1$.

To detect one error, the code must have a weight of at least 2. To detect two errors, the code must have a weight of at least 3. To correct one error, the code must have a weight of at least 3, and to correct two errors, the weight of the code must be at least 5.

To detect	The weight must be
1 error	2
2 errors	3
.	.
.	.
.	.
k errors	$k + 1$

To correct	The weight must be
1 error	3
2 errors	5
.	.
.	.
k errors	$2k + 1$

Returning to the problem of devising a code for the two-bit messages {00, 01, 10, 11}, we must construct a binary linear code with a weight of 3. One method is

to use what are called *parity-check sums*.

A binary string is said to be of *even parity* if the sum of its bits is even and of *odd parity* if the sum of its bits is odd. For example, 0010110 has odd parity, whereas 1010110 has even parity.

Using the idea of parity, suppose that we add three additional digits, called parity-check bits, to our message bits so that the code word will be of the form $m_1 m_2 p_1 p_2 p_3$, where m_1 and m_2 are the message bits and p_1, p_2, and p_3 are the parity-check bits. For this first example, we choose p_1 as a parity check on m_1, p_2 as a parity check on m_2, and p_3 as a parity check on the sum of m_1 and m_2. That is, we choose p_1, p_2, and p_3 so that

$$m_1 + p_1 = 0,$$
$$m_2 + p_2 = 0,$$

and

$$m_1 + m_2 + p_3 = 0.$$

To form code words from message words, some combinations of the message digits are used to form parity-check digits.

Example:
The message to be sent is
$$m_1 m_2.$$
The message with parity-check bits added is
$$m_1 m_2 p_1 p_2 p_3.$$
To send the message
$$m_1 m_2 = 10,$$

$$1 + p_1 = 0 \qquad \rightarrow \qquad p_1 = 1,$$
$$0 + p_2 = 0 \qquad \rightarrow \qquad p_2 = 0,$$
$$1 + 0 + p_3 = 0 \qquad \rightarrow \qquad p_3 = 1.$$

The code word for 10 becomes
$$m_1 m_2 p_1 p_2 p_3 = 10101.$$

Using this scheme, we encode our four message words as follows:

$00 \rightarrow 00000$ $01 \rightarrow 01011$

$10 \rightarrow 10101$ $11 \rightarrow 11110$

The list below shows each code word and the five possible messages that are a distance of 1 from that word.

00000	10000, 01000, 00100, 00010, 00001
01011	11011, 00011, 01111, 01001, 01010
10101	00101, 11101, 10001, 10111, 10100
11110	01110, 10110, 11010, 11100, 11111

If any of these messages is received, it will be decoded as the corresponding code word. However, there are 2^5, or thirty-two, possible five-bit messages, and we have accounted for only twenty-four of them. This leaves eight other messages that are a distance of at least 2 from any of our code words. If one of those eight messages is received, we assume that some error has occurred, but the error is not correctable.

✔ **Your Understanding:**

3. Find the other eight possible five-bit messages. Show that the distance between each of these and the four code words is at least 2.

4. The picture below is composed of eight shades of gray. The eight shades are each assigned a binary code according to the chart below the picture. Use parity-check bits to design a code for these eight shades of gray that will correct all one-bit errors. You will need three parity-check bits. Remember to check the following:

   • Your code should have weight 3.

   • Your code words should form a binary linear code, that is, the sum of any two code words is another code word.

   Write your results in the table.

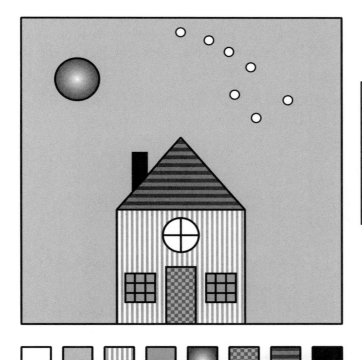

Message	Code Word	Weight
000		
001		
010		
011		
100		
101		
110		
111		

000   001   010   011   100   101   110   111

Hamming Codes

Richard Hamming, a mathematician at Bell Laboratories, developed an infinite set of single-error correcting, double-error detecting codes in the late 1940s. His work laid a foundation for error-correction techniques that have become increasingly useful with the growth of digital technology. Satellite communication, home computers, fax machines, compact discs, cellular telephones, digital audiotape, and digital television are just a few examples of technologies that use error-correcting codes. There is an elegant way to derive the Hamming codes using matrices, which leads to an easy method for finding and correcting errors in received messages.

Hamming developed codes that work in certain situations. These codes can be described when there are m parity-check digits and $n = 2^m - 1 - m$ message digits. We first examine codes for special values of m and n and later look at codes for any value of n.

If $m = 2$, then $n = 2^2 - 1 - 2 = 1$ message digit.

If $m = 3$, then $n = 2^3 - 1 - 3 = 4$ message digits.

If $m = 4$, then $n = 2^4 - 1 - 4 = 11$ message digits.

Parity-check Digits (m)	Message Digits (n)
2	1
3	4
4	11
⋮	⋮
m	$2^m - 1 - m$

You can develop a Hamming code by following these procedures:

(i) Form a matrix, H, with m rows and $2^m - 1$ columns. The columns of the matrix are the binary representations of the integers $1, 2, 3, ..., (2^m - 1)$. The matrices for $m = 2, 3,$ and 4 are shown below with the decimal integers written above the columns.

$$H_2 = \begin{matrix} 1\,2\,3 \\ \begin{bmatrix} 0 & 1 & 1 \\ 1 & 0 & 1 \end{bmatrix} \end{matrix} \qquad H_3 = \begin{matrix} 1\,2\,3\,4\,5\,6\,7 \\ \begin{bmatrix} 0 & 0 & 0 & 1 & 1 & 1 & 1 \\ 0 & 1 & 1 & 0 & 0 & 1 & 1 \\ 1 & 0 & 1 & 0 & 1 & 0 & 1 \end{bmatrix} \end{matrix}$$

$$H_4 = \begin{matrix} 1\,\ 2\,\ 3\,\ 4\,\ 5\,\ 6\,\ 7\,\ 8\,\ 9\ 10\ 11\ 12\,13\,14\,15 \\ \begin{bmatrix} 0 & 0 & 0 & 0 & 0 & 0 & 0 & 1 & 1 & 1 & 1 & 1 & 1 & 1 & 1 \\ 0 & 0 & 0 & 1 & 1 & 1 & 1 & 0 & 0 & 0 & 0 & 1 & 1 & 1 & 1 \\ 0 & 1 & 1 & 0 & 0 & 1 & 1 & 0 & 0 & 1 & 1 & 0 & 0 & 1 & 1 \\ 1 & 0 & 1 & 0 & 1 & 0 & 1 & 0 & 1 & 0 & 1 & 0 & 1 & 0 & 1 \end{bmatrix} \end{matrix}$$

(ii) Write an $(m + n) \times 1$ matrix U whose elements are the n message digits and the m parity-check digits. The message digits are represented by $w_1, w_2, ..., w_n$ and the parity-check digits are $p_1, p_2, ..., p_m$. Locate the columns of H that have only one 1 in them and write the parity-check symbols in the corresponding rows of U. Write the w_i in the remaining rows of U. We use $m = 3$ as an example for the rest of the development of the code. The parity-check bits are written in rows 1, 2, and 4 of U because these columns of H each have a single 1. The message bits go in the other rows of U.

$$U = \begin{bmatrix} p_1 \\ p_2 \\ w_1 \\ p_3 \\ w_2 \\ w_3 \\ w_4 \end{bmatrix}$$

(iii) If the message $p_1 p_2 w_1 p_3 w_2 w_3 w_4$ is received correctly, the product HU will be equal to the null matrix because we are working with even parity. This equation $HU = 0$ gives the parity-check equations.

$$H_3U = \begin{bmatrix} 0001111 \\ 0110011 \\ 1010101 \end{bmatrix} \begin{bmatrix} p_1 \\ p_2 \\ w_1 \\ p_3 \\ w_2 \\ w_3 \\ w_4 \end{bmatrix} = \begin{bmatrix} 0 \\ 0 \\ 0 \end{bmatrix}$$

$p_3 + w_2 + w_3 + w_4 = 0$ $p_3 = w_2 + w_3 + w_4$

$p_2 + w_1 + w_3 + w_4 = 0$ or $p_2 = w_1 + w_3 + w_4$

$p_1 + w_1 + w_2 + w_4 = 0$ $p_1 = w_1 + w_2 + w_4$

These equations can be used to encode the message. For example, let's encode 1011.

$w_1 = 1$ $w_2 = 0$ $w_3 = 1$ $w_4 = 1$

$w_{1\,+}\,w_{2\,+}\,w_4 = 1 + 0 + 1 = 0 \rightarrow p_1 = 0$

$w_{1\,+}\,w_{3\,+}\,w_4 = 1 + 1 + 1 = 1 \rightarrow p_2 = 1$

$w_{2\,+}\,w_{3\,+}\,w_4 = 0 + 1 + 1 = 0 \rightarrow p_3 = 0$

The message $1011 \rightarrow 0110011$, and the encoding is completed.

✔ Your Understanding:

5. Use the parity-check equations to complete the following encoding table for the sixteen possible four-bit messages.

Message	Code Word	Message	Code Word
0000		1000	
0001		1001	
0010		1010	
0011		1011	0110011
0100		1100	
0101		1101	
0110		1110	
0111		1111	

The format of the code word that is used here is different from the other codes we have developed using parity-check equations. The other codes had the message bits at the beginning of the code word and the parity bits appended to the mes-

sage. Here the parity-check bits are intermingled with the message bits, which makes it somewhat more difficult to read—for a human, but not for a computer. The reason for writing the code word this way is to make decoding much more convenient. The codes generated here can be shown to be equivalent to the codes in which the message bits were listed first.

Decoding with the Hamming Matrix

The parity-check matrix, H, is useful in decoding a received message. Let r be a received message written in matrix form. For example, suppose that the received message is 0110111. Then r is the matrix shown at the right.

$$r = \begin{bmatrix} 0 \\ 1 \\ 1 \\ 0 \\ 1 \\ 1 \\ 1 \end{bmatrix}$$

The matrix product $H \cdot r$ is called the *syndrome* for the message. If $H \cdot r = 0$, the message is correct; if $H \cdot r \neq 0$, an error has occurred and the syndrome indicates which bit is in error. In the case of the received message 0110111,

$$H_3 r = \begin{bmatrix} 0001111 \\ 0110011 \\ 1010101 \end{bmatrix} \begin{bmatrix} 0 \\ 1 \\ 1 \\ 0 \\ 1 \\ 1 \\ 1 \end{bmatrix} = \begin{bmatrix} 1 \\ 0 \\ 1 \end{bmatrix}.$$

Note that the syndrome corresponds to the fifth column of H_3. When a single error has been made, the syndrome will always point to a column of H. It is in this position that the error has been made. But remember that we made the fifth column of H be the integer 5 in binary notation, so it is not necessary to compare the syndrome with the columns of H to find where the error occurred. All that must be done is to convert the syndrome to its base-ten form.

$$101 = 1(4) + 0(2) + 1(1) = 5$$

To correct the message, we go to the fifth position, change the 1 to a 0, and have the corrected message, 0110011.

Fifth Digit
↓

| 0 | 1 | 1 | 0 | 1 | 1 | 1 | Received Message |
| 0 | 1 | 1 | 0 | 0 | 1 | 1 | Corrected Message |

✔ **Your Understanding:**

Use the matrix H_3 to decode the following messages:

$$H_3 = \begin{bmatrix} 0001111 \\ 0110011 \\ 1010101 \end{bmatrix}$$

6. 1101011   7. 0011001
8. 0100110   9. 1111110

10. *Challenge:* Develop the parity-check matrices for a Hamming code with eleven message bits and four parity-check bits. Do not attempt to encode all the messages. How many possible messages exist with eleven message bits?

Using Hamming Codes to Derive Other Codes

The Hamming code we just created is called a *perfect code* because it has the property that every possible received message is a distance of 1 from one and only one code word. These perfect Hamming codes exist only when the number of parity-check bits is m and the number of message bits is $n = 2m - 1 - m$. However, it is possible to obtain good, but not perfect, single-error–correcting codes for any value of n by deleting certain columns of the matrix H.

Suppose that we want a single-bit error-correcting code for $n = 2$ message digits. We saw earlier that two parity-check bits are needed to correct one-digit messages, whereas three parity-check bits give single-bit error correction for four message digits. Since $1 \leq 2 \leq 4$, we need the

Hamming code matrix for $m = 3$. But since our message contains only two message digits, we need to transmit $m + n = 3 + 2 = 5$ bits: three parity-check digits and two message digits. To accomplish this, we use the matrix H_3 and delete the last two columns so that the new matrix H has three rows and five columns. Form HU as before and find the parity-check equations.

$$HU = \begin{bmatrix} 00011 \\ 01100 \\ 10101 \end{bmatrix} \begin{bmatrix} p_1 \\ p_2 \\ w_1 \\ p_3 \\ w_2 \end{bmatrix} = \begin{bmatrix} 0 \\ 0 \\ 0 \end{bmatrix}$$

$$p_3 + w_2 = 0$$
$$p_2 + w_1 = 0$$
$$p_1 + w_1 + w_2 = 0$$

The encoding table for this code is shown at the right. Compare this code with the five-bit code that was generated earlier using the code word $m_1 m_2 p_1 p_2 p_3$. Are the parity-check equations the same?

Message	Code Word
00	00000
01	10011
10	11100
11	01111

$Hr = 0 \rightarrow$ The message is correct.

$Hr \neq 0 \rightarrow$ An error has occurred.

To decode a received message, we proceed as we did before by forming the matrix r where r is the received message written in matrix form. We then check the syndrome, Hr. If the syndrome corresponds to a column of H, correct the bit that is in error. If the syndrome does not correspond to a column of H, an uncorrectable error has occurred.

Even though this code is not a perfect code, it can be shown that it is the best single-error–correcting code we can get for two message bits and three parity-check bits. To see why a perfect code cannot be obtained for two message bits, consider that there are four code words and that for each code word, there are five possible messages that are at a distance of 1 from that code word. For example, the messages

10000, 01000, 00100, 00010, and 00001

are distance 1 from 00000. The twenty messages that are at distance 1 from a code word, together with the four code words, account for only twenty-four of the thirty-two possible five-digit messages. Thus, eight of the possible thirty-two messages are at a distance greater than 1 from any code word. When one of those eight messages is received, decoding it is not possible. Codes for other values of n message digits can be similarly generated by omitting appropriate columns from the Hamming code matrix.

✔ Your Understanding:

11. Use the foregoing technique to generate a single-error–correcting code for three message bits.

12. Use the foregoing technique to generate a single-error–correcting code for five message bits.

Application: Long-Distance Tic-Tac-Toe

Suppose that you have become acquainted with a friendly E.T. who is visiting Earth. One day, after you learn to communicate with E.T., you decide to teach her to play tic-tac-toe. She thinks that this game is so much fun that she wants to continue to play even after she returns to her home planet. To make that possible, you each buy a binary transmitter-receiver capable of communicating between the planets. Use what you have learned about error-correcting codes and data compression to devise an efficient code for sending your tic-tac-toe move to E.T.

Application: Speeding Your Mail with ZIP + 4

The United States Postal Service uses a binary bar code, together with a check digit for detecting errors, to encode five-digit ZIP codes and the more recent nine-digit "ZIP + 4" codes. This bar code, which can be read by scanning machines, helps speed the sorting of mail.

Each digit in a ZIP code is encoded with five binary digits, or bars, where the short bars in the code represent 0's and the long bars represent 1's. A five-digit ZIP code consists of thirty-two bars that encode the five digits of the ZIP code plus one check digit; the ZIP + 4 bar code has fifty-two bars to encode the nine-digit ZIP code and one check digit. The bar codes always begin and end with a long bar or 1; these bars, called *guard bars,* signal that a code is enclosed between them. The check digit, also consisting of five bars, is chosen so that all digits in the code have a sum that is a multiple of 10.

Note: Some ZIP code bar codes now have twelve digits rather than ten. These digits are the nine-digit ZIP + 4 number followed by the last two digits of the street address or box number and a check digit chosen so that the sum of all twelve digits is evenly divisible by 10.

The nine patterns below correspond to the ZIP codes listed. Break the code and identify the pattern that corresponds to each ZIP code.

(a) ‖ııı‖ıı‖ıı‖ıı‖ı‖ı‖ıı‖ı‖ı‖ıı‖	_____90210
(b) ‖ııı‖ıı‖ı‖ı‖ıı‖ıı‖ı‖ı‖ı‖ı	_____53981
(c) ‖ıı‖ı‖‖ı‖ıı‖ıı‖ı‖ı‖ıı‖‖ı‖ı	_____69794
(d) ‖‖ıııı‖‖ı‖ıı‖ıı‖ı‖ıı‖‖ıı‖ı‖‖	_____12882
(e) ‖ı‖ıı‖‖ıııı‖ı‖ıı‖‖‖ıı‖ıı‖ı‖ı	_____78964
(f) ‖ı‖ıı‖ı‖ı‖ı‖‖ıııı‖ı‖ı‖‖ıııı‖‖‖	_____39048
(g) ‖ıı‖‖ı‖ı‖ıı‖‖ıııı‖ıı‖‖ı‖ıı‖‖ıı‖	_____29857
(h) ‖ı‖‖ıı‖ı‖ı‖ıı‖ıı‖‖ı‖ıı‖ıı‖ı‖ı‖ı	_____45046
(i) ‖ı‖ı‖ııı‖‖ı‖ı‖ıı‖ıı‖ıııı‖‖ı‖ıı‖‖	_____03823

1. Enter the bar code and the corresponding binary code for each digit.

Decimal Digit	Bar Code	Binary Code
1		
2		
3		
4		
5		
6		
7		
8		
9		
0		

Identify the following ZIP + 4 bar codes:

(a) ‖ıı‖ı‖ıı‖‖‖ıı‖‖ıııı‖‖ı‖ı‖ı‖ı‖ıı‖ı‖ıı‖‖ıı‖ı‖ı

(b) ‖ı‖ıı‖‖ı‖ıı‖ı‖ı‖ı‖ı‖ıı‖ı‖ı‖ıı‖‖ı‖ı‖ıı‖ıı‖‖ı‖ı

(c) ‖ı‖ı‖ıı‖ı‖ıı‖ı‖ıı‖‖ı‖ıı‖ıı‖‖‖ı‖ıııı‖‖ı‖‖ıı‖ı‖ıı‖

(d) ‖ı‖‖ıı‖ıı‖ıııı‖‖ıı‖‖ı‖ıı‖‖‖ıııı‖‖ıı‖‖ıııı‖ı‖ıı‖‖‖

(e) ‖ı‖ı‖ıı‖‖ıı‖ı‖ı‖ı‖‖ı‖ıı‖‖‖‖ıııı‖ı‖ı‖ıı‖ıı‖‖‖

(f) ‖‖ı‖ıı‖ıı‖‖‖ıııı‖‖ı‖ı‖ıı‖‖‖‖ıı‖‖ıı‖‖ıı‖ı‖ı

(g) ‖ıı‖‖ıı‖ı‖‖ı‖ıı‖ıı‖‖ı‖‖ıııı‖‖ı‖ı‖ı‖ı‖‖ıııı‖‖

(h) ‖ı‖ı‖ıı‖ı‖‖‖ıı‖ı‖ıııı‖‖ıı‖‖ı‖ı‖ı‖ı‖ıııı‖‖ı‖ı‖ı

(i) ‖ı‖‖ıııı‖‖‖ıı‖‖ı‖ıı‖‖ıııı‖ı‖ı‖ı‖ı‖ıı‖ı‖‖‖ıııı‖‖ı‖ı

2. Each ZIP code bar code below has one error. Find the correct ZIP code.

(a) ‖ı‖ıı‖‖ıııı‖‖ıı‖ıııı‖‖ıı‖ı‖‖ı‖ıııı‖‖ıı‖ıııı‖ıııı‖‖‖ı‖

(b) ‖ı‖‖ıı‖‖ıııı‖‖ı‖ıı‖ıı‖‖‖‖ıııı‖ı‖ıı‖ıı‖‖ı‖ı‖ı‖ı‖ı‖ı‖ı

3. The ZIP + 4 code for the NASA Marshall Space Flight Center, Huntsville, Alabama is 35812-0001. Write a bar code for this ZIP code. Don't forget to include the check digit.

4. Study the error-detecting and error-correcting capabilities of the ZIP code bar code.

(*a*) Can it detect, correct, or detect and correct two errors in the same block of five bars?

(*b*) Can it detect, correct, or detect and correct two errors in different blocks of five bars?

(*c*) Can it detect the transposition of digits in a ZIP code, for example, detect 47812-9956 instead of 47821-9956?

Extension: The following topics are recommended for further study about codes used in everyday life:

• The ISBN code used internationally for books

• The UPC code used by merchandisers to code products for sale

• The codes used by banks, airlines, automobile manufacturers, and parcel-delivery services, and the Soundex code used for genealogical research

RESOURCES FOR FURTHER STUDY

Brogdon, Bill. "Space-Age Trail Blazers." *Outdoor Life,* August 1993, 53–55.

Chien, Philip. "You Are Here." *Popular Mechanics,* November 1993, 50–52.

COMAP. *For All Practical Purposes: Introduction to Contemporary Mathematics,* 3rd. ed. New York: W. H. Freeman & Co., 1994.

———. *Cracking the Code.* Lexington, Mass.: Video Applications Library, COMAP, 1993.

———. *Geometry: New Tools for New Technologies.* Lexington, Mass.: Video Applications Library, COMAP, 1993.

Dossey, John A., et al. *Discrete Mathematics,* 2nd ed. New York: Harper Collins College Publishers, 1993.

DuPont, Al. *Visual-eye-zing Orbital Spaceflight around the Earth.* Houston, Tex.: NASA, Lyndon B. Johnson Space Center, 1994.

Gordon, Sheldon, et al. *Functioning in the Real World.* Reading, Mass.: Addison-Wesley Publishing Co., 1995.

Grimaldi, Ralph P. *Discrete and Combinatorial Mathematics: An Applied Introduction,* 3rd ed. Reading, Mass.: Addison-Wesley Publishing Co., 1994.

Haynes, Robert. *How We Get Pictures from Space.* Washington, D.C.: NASA, 1987.

Herring, Thomas A. "The Global Positioning System." *Scientific American,* February 1996, 44–50.

Hurn, Jeff. *Differential GPS Explained.* Sunnyvale, Calif.: Trimble Navigation Limited, 1993.

———. *GPS: A Guide to the Next Utility.* Sunnyvale, Calif.: Trimble Navigation Limited, 1989.

Johnson, Torrence V. "The Galileo Mission." *Scientific American,* December 1995, 44–51.

Kastner, Bernice. *Space Mathematics—a Resource for Secondary School Teachers.* Washington, D.C.: NASA, 1985.

Langley, Richard B. "GPS and the Internet." *GPS World,* November 1995.

———. "A GPS Glossary." *GPS World,* October 1995.

Lee, Wayne. *To Rise from Earth.* Austin, Tex.: Texas Space Grant Consortium, 1994.

Malkevitch, Joseph, Gary Froelich, and Daniel Froelich. *Codes Galore.* Lexington, Mass.: COMAP, 1993.

———. *Loads of Codes.* Lexington, Mass.: COMAP, 1993.

Markwart, Andy. "A Precision Farmer's Plan for 1996." *Prairie Farmer,* December 1995.

Murdock, Jerald, et al. *Advanced Algebra through Data Exploration: A Graphing Calculator Approach.* Berkeley, Calif.: Key Curriculum Press, 1997.

Peterson, W. Wesley, and E. J. Weldon, Jr. *Error-Correcting Codes,* 2nd ed. Cambridge, Mass.: MIT Press, 1972.

Sagan, Carl. *Cosmos.* New York: Ballantine Books, 1980.

Space Based Astronomy. Washington, D.C.: NASA, 1994.

Vest, Floyd, and Raymond Benge. "Latitude and Longitude." *Consortium* (winter 1994–95).

Vest, Floyd, William Diedrich, and Kenneth Vos. "Mathematics and the Global Positioning System." *Consortium* (spring 1994).

Wright, Ed. "GPS Takes a Vacation." *GPS World,* June 1995, 22–30.

APPENDIX A
NASA RESOURCES FOR EDUCATORS

NASA's Central Operation of Resources for Educators (CORE) was established for the national and international distribution of NASA-produced educational materials in audiovisual format. Educators can obtain a catalog and an order form by one of the following methods:

- NASA CORE
  Lorain County Joint Vocational School
  15181 Route 58 South
  Oberlin, OH 44074
- Phone (216) 774-1051, ext. 249 or 293
- Fax (216) 774-2144
- E-mail nasaco@leeca8.leeca.ohio.gov
- Home Page: http://spacelink.msfc.nasa.gov/CORE

Educators Resource Center Network

To make additional information available to the education community, the NASA Education Division has created the NASA Educators Resource Center (ERC) network. ERCs contain a wealth of information for educators: publications, reference books, slide sets, audio cassettes, videotapes, telelecture programs, computer programs, lesson plans, and teacher guides with activities. Teachers may preview, copy, or receive NASA materials at these sites. Because each NASA Field Center has its own areas of expertise, no two ERCs are exactly alike. Phone calls are welcome if you are unable to visit the ERC that serves your geographic area. A list of the centers and the regions they serve is at the right.

Regional Educators Resource Centers (RERCs) offer more educators access to NASA educational materials. NASA has formed partnerships with universities, museums, and other educational institutions to serve as RERCs in many states. A complete list of RERCs is available through CORE, or electronically via NASA Spacelink.

NASA Spacelink is an electronic information system designed to provide current educational information to teachers, faculty, and students. Spacelink offers a wide range of computer text files, software, and graphics related to aeronautics and space programs. The system may be accessed by computer through direct-dial modem or the Internet.

For more information, contact: NASA Spacelink, Education Programs Office, Mail Code CL01, NASA Marshall Space Flight Center, Huntsville, AL 35812-0001.
Voice phone: (205) 961-1225 • E-mail: comments@spacelink.msfc.nasa.gov

NASA Television (NTV) is the Agency's distribution system for live and taped programs. It offers the public a front-row seat for launches and missions, as well as informational and educational programming, historical documentaries, and updates on the latest developments in aeronautics and space science.

For more information on NASA Television, contact:
NASA Headquarters, Code P-2, NASA TV, Washington, DC 20546-0001
Phone: (202) 358-3572
Home Page: http://www.hq.nasa.gov/office/pao/ntv.html

For more information about the Education Satellite Videoconference Series, contact: Videoconference Producer, NASA Teaching from Space Program, 308 CITD, Room A, Oklahoma State University, Stillwater, OK 74078-8089
E-mail: edge@aesp.nasa.okstate.edu
Home Page: http://www.okstate.edu/aespVC.html

The brochure *How to Access NASA's Education Materials and Services,* EP-1996-09-345-HQ, serves as a guide to accessing a variety of NASA materials and services for educators. Copies are available through the ERC network, or electronically via NASA Spacelink.

AK, AZ, CA, HI, ID, MT, NV, OR, UT, WA, WY
NASA Educators Resource Center
Mail Stop 253-2
NASA Ames Research Center
Moffet Field, CA 94035-1000
Phone: (415) 604-3574

CT, DE, DC, ME, MD, MA, NH, NJ, NY, PA, RI, VT
NASA Educators Resource Center
Mail Code 130.3
NASA Goddard Space Flight Center
Greenbelt, MD 20771-0001
Phone: (301) 286-8570

CO, KS, NE, NM, ND, OK, SD, TX
NASA Educators Resource Center
Mail Code AP2
NASA Johnson Space Center
2101 NASA Road One
Houston, TX 77058-3696
Phone: (281) 483-8696

FL, GA, PR, VI
NASA Educators Resource Center
Mail Code ERL
NASA Kennedy Space Center
Kennedy Space Center, FL 32899-0001
Phone: (407) 867-4090

KY, NC, SC, VA, WV
Virginia Air and Space Museum
NASA Educators Resource Center for
  NASA Langley Research Center
600 Settler's Landing Road
Hampton, VA 23669-4033
Phone: (757) 727-0900 x 757

IL IN, MI, MN, OH, WI
NASA Educators Resource Center
Mail Stop 8-1
NASA Lewis Research Center
21000 Brookpark Road
Cleveland, OH 44135-3191
Phone: (216) 433-2017

AL, AR, IA, LA, MO, TN
U.S. Space and Rocket Center
NASA Educators Resource Center for
  NASA Marshall Space Flight Center
P. O. Box 070015
Huntsville, AL 35807-7015
Phone: (205) 544-5812

MS
NASA Educators Resource Center
Building 1200
NASA John C. Stennis Space Center
Stennis Space Center, MS 39529-6000
Phone: (601) 688-3338

Serves inquiries related to space and planetary exploration
NASA Educators Resource Center
JPL Educational Outreach
Mail Stop CS-530
NASA Jet Propulsion Laboratory
4800 Oak Grove Drive
Pasadena, CA 91109-8099
Phone: (818) 354-6916

CA cities near the center
NASA Educators Resource Center for
  NASA Dryden Flight Research Center
45108 North Third Street East
Lancaster, CA 93535
Phone: (805) 948-7347

VA and MD's Eastern Shores
NASA Educators Resource Center
Education Complex—Visitor Center
Building J-1
NASA Wallops Flight Facility
Wallops Island, VA 23337-5099
Phone: (757) 824-2297/2298